ALL LOVE - A BIOGRAPHY OF RIDLEY HERSCHELL

Geoffrey Henderson

Published by HTS Media

Copyright © 2006 by Geoffrey Henderson

All rights reserved.

ISBN 978-0-9555304-0-1

Printed in the United Kingdom

For further information contact Geoffrey Henderson at info@htsmedia.com

Dedication

To my wife Carole for her support
and because she came to love Ridley and Helen.

FOREWORD

It is always inspiring to read about the lives of fellow believers.

Like many other peoples, we Jews love to hear stories about life: we like telling stories and we like listening to stories.

So it was with great interest that I started to read this fascinating and beautifully written account of the life of Ridley Herschell, who was born two hundred years ago.

It is not difficult to see in Ridley Herschell a life that is inspiring and encouraging.

We marvel at how God works His wonderful purpose out over the centuries; we see similarities between his experiences and our own.

You will also discover in this book a particular poignancy. How moving it is that Geoffrey's great great Grandfather was saved through Ridley Herschell's ministry!

How amazing the gospel is, and how wonderfully God works these things out in our lives. Who knows what repercussions there will be when we share the good news in the power of the Spirit?

One thing is sure: God's Word never returns to Him void without accomplishing that for which He has sent it. What an encouragement that is to us, who 200 years on, still seek to proclaim that same gospel. We are involved in the same struggle; we have in our hearts that same elusive goal that one day, even one day soon, Israel will come to know her Messiah and glorious Lord. What a day that will be!

Life unfolds much like a story with all its different chapters, its dramas, loves, hopes, joys, tears and sorrows. There is cohesion to events we can't fully see. It is only when these are pieced together, sometimes even after a person has died, that we understand more fully the beautiful unseen fabric of the life that God has given us.

Thank you Geoffrey. You have has done us a real service in going to such lengths, and in searching out so many interesting aspects of Ridley and Helen Herschell's life.

For those of us who have been captivated by the Jewish Jesus, and who share a concern for His chosen people, this book has to be mandatory reading.

Stuart Cohen

March 5th 2007

Chapter 1

It is a melancholy truth that even great men have their poor relations.

Charles Dickens, *Bleak House*

I'd never spoken to a real Baron before. I was quite excited as the phone began to ring deep in the Oxfordshire countryside. I wondered if a stooped, ageing butler might answer. Or perhaps a maid wearing a black and white uniform would pick up an old GPO handset in the library and say, "Lord Herschell's residence, his Lordship is away on business in Africa for several years. May I help you?"

My fantasy was shattered as the digital phones connected, and the friendly voice of Rognvald Richard Farrer Herschell, the third Baron Herschell of Durham simply said, "Hello"… just like anybody else.

"Lord Herschell?" I said.

"Yes", said the Baron, probably wondering who else I thought it might be.

"I'm doing some research on the life of your great-grandfather and I wondered if you might be able to answer one or two questions for me."

I really had about ten thousand questions, but I didn't want to push my luck at this stage. I was actually talking to Ridley Herschell's great grandson and I didn't want to lose him.

"I don't know very much", said his Lordship with a drawling upper class accent which lived up to my expectations of an hereditary peer, "I was only six when he died, you know."

"Yes, I know", I said, immediately regretting the presumption of intimacy with the details of his family life, which I'd only got from the public library anyway.

He thought for a moment, and then said vaguely, "I've got a couple of rather boring books he wrote on the partition of Venezuela, everything else was lost in the fire in London years ago."

My heart sank. This wasn't looking good. I'd never been much of a researcher, and now the entire archives of the Herschell family seemed to have gone up in smoke before I'd even started. "Wait a minute", I thought as I desperately counted the generations, I hadn't read anything about this Venezuelan connection. Were we talking about the same Herschell?

"I'm sorry", I mumbled as I scribbled an instant genealogy on my notepad, "I'm talking about your great grandfather, the Reverend Ridley Herschell?"

Short silence. "Oh, well I can't really tell you much at all about him, apart from what you can find out for yourself. What's your connection with him, anyway?"

"He converted my great-great-grandfather to Christianity back in the 1830s when he was an evangelist in Southend. They became good friends.

"Interesting", said the noble lord, "you must be as old as me, then."

"No, no", I said, re-checking the instant family tree, "My great-great grandfather." "Oh, I see", said his Lordship, politely losing interest.

I thanked him for his time and slipped happily back into my fantasy world of an upper class English gent absent-mindedly stroking a faithful gundog. It was all a long way from Poland and the freezing white river banks of the Vistula.

Chapter 2

Who should we get conquered by...
Germany...Russia...Germany...Russia.
Napoleon come save us!
Anonymous

Poland - April 1807

The long road from Friedland to Warsaw crosses the great River Vistula at Torun. Thirty miles to the south lies the small Polish town of Strzelno, home to Rabbi Hillel, his son-in-law Judah, Judah's wife Ghetal, their daughter and two sons. Judah had been married to Ghetal for six years, and now they were expecting their fourth child.

Twelve years had passed since the final military partition of Poland by the unholy alliance of Russia, Austria and Prussia. In the share-out of the spoils Prussia had got the mediaeval town of Torun[1] and Poland had ceased to exist as an independent state.

It was early Spring, 1807, and Napoleon Bonaparte's exhausted *Grande Armée* was resting up before heading east, across what was left of a devastated Poland. The newly acquired Prussian territory was to become part of the mighty French Empire and not, contrary to promises made to the Polish people, a newly liberated Poland.

For now, the Emperor had put his army into winter quarters. The elite cavalry were posted in the towns and villages along the valley of the Vistula, from Torun to the Baltic. Little Strzelno had become a garrison town.

As he struggled through the busy streets and across the square, avoiding

---

[1] German Thorn

the horses and the stares of the young French soldiers, Rabbi Hillel, grey-bearded, head covered in a thick fur hat, and wrapped in black against the bitter cold, had little enough interest in either the French or the Prussians. Foreign invasions and occupations were not new to him or his people in Strzelno. But, even though they had seen it all before and they were far enough from the fighting to feel as safe as they could ever feel, most other Jews had left for the city, in spite of legal restrictions on where they could move. There were now only four Jewish families left in Strzelno.

But the Rabbi had more important and more joyful things on his mind that day. A grandchild was to be born, maybe another grandson to follow in his own footsteps, or maybe he'd take on the family business of his father. But where was the father? Where was Judah of Strzelno as he was still known in this small Jewish community? Judah, like generations before him was a successful brewer and distiller and urgent business had called him to the great city of Warsaw, 140 miles to the east. But communications were poor, or even non-existent. The invention of the telegraph was still thirty years away and the first railway station in the region of Poznań wouldn't be built for another forty years. Travel was hard and almost impossible at times when the long dark winter set in. The rough roads were blocked by troops and equipment, or impassable with the slowly melting winter snow. Spring came late to Poland in 1807 and Napoleon himself, writing home to Josephine described the weather as "wretched."[2]

Rabbi Hillel was heading for the family home where his daughter was confined to bed for the forthcoming birth. Everybody knew the Rabbi's daughter Ghetal; a pillar of the Jewish community and a woman of great faith. She had put her trust in the God of Abraham, Isaac and Jacob many times and he'd always brought her through. She had stayed in Strzelno rather than risk travelling with the child being due so soon. But when the soldiers lit a large blazing fire in the street close by she was frightened. It was too close to the houses, much too close. She could feel the heat on her face as the shadow of the bright dancing flames flickered on the ceiling where she lay.

---

[2] *The Corsican: A Diary of Napoleon's Life in His Own Words*, R. M. Johnston, 1910

Psalm 46 ran around her head, "God is our refuge and strength, an ever-present help in trouble." The soldiers really didn't seem to care. They were a long way from home. There was no telling what they might do next, not only to the Jews but to the whole town. "Therefore we are unafraid, even if the earth gives way, even if the mountains tumble into the depths of the sea."

Ghetal's mind was racing, she was very afraid now. Sporadic cannon fire came from somewhere in the distance, deep, threatening thuds disturbing the still cold air. Perhaps she should have left. Perhaps she should have gone with Judah to Warsaw. Nobody was safe here in this distant outpost of the European battlefield, "…though its waters roar and foam and the mountains quake with their surging." The familiar words of Scripture brought her some peace. She rested briefly, laid her head back on the pillow and sighed. For a time the guns fell silent. What did they want, these French invaders? Was their own country not big enough for them? Ghetal drifted in and out of a restless, fitful sleep. We Jews had a country of our own once, she thought, far away across the mountains, over the fearful Mediterranean Sea. A country much smaller than theirs, yet fruits more luscious than any in the fields of France grew in the warm spring sunshine of the land of Israel. And the sleeping deserts of the Patriarchs, full of Covenant promise, still waited quietly to blossom into rainbow colours for the new children of Israel.

And then, without warning, it happened. Another explosion, nearer this time, much nearer. The bedroom window disintegrated and flew towards her. The whole room seemed to collapse, engulfing her in blinding smoke and bitter dust. Plaster flew from the walls like musket rounds and for a moment the whole house trembled.

A cannonball, small but horrifically destructive in the little bedroom had crashed into the wall beside the head of Ghetal's bed, and grey dust now covered her entire body. Her father entered the house and rushed to the room. Had she been hit? What about the baby! Was the town under attack? Were all the Jews to be wiped out?

Dust settled on his grey beard and an icy wind blew through the shattered window frame. The cannonball had entered through the small window of her room and struck the wall with such force that Ghetal was momentarily unconscious. Rabbi Hillel prayed with all his heart. Ghetal stirred and clung to him, unable even to cry out. Where was Judah, where were her sons. Oh why hadn't they moved on with the others? The Jews must always move on, keeping ahead of the troubles, the deportations. Together they waited for the next shot, Ghetal closed her eyes. They waited and waited, but it never came. The fire burned on in the streets, throwing bright red sparks into the grey sky. The young soldiers shouted and swore in their unfamiliar language. Darkness fell, but the shots never came.

Whether the cannon had been fired in that direction intentionally nobody ever knew. Where the missile had come from nobody ever found out. Artillery fire was often heard in the distance, but never that close. Perhaps it was an accident during a practice. Perhaps not. But no one dared to ask. Nobody ever asked the French authorities.

Perhaps the words of the prophet Obadiah were in the Rabbi's mind as he began to pick at the rubble:

"But on Mount Zion will be deliverance; it will be holy, and the house of Jacob will possess its inheritance."[3]

Years later one of Ghetal's sons would recall: "To the very end of her life mother often related to us, with the deepest thankfulness, how the dear Lord had carried her through all her danger and distress; and then exhorted us also to put our trust in God."

And the faithful Ghetal would often recall the words of Psalm 50:
"…and call upon me in the day of trouble; I will deliver you, and you will honour me."[4]

In spite of everything the child was safely delivered on Tuesday 7th April 1807. A boy, a third son. Judah still wasn't back when Ghetal named the child after a long departed relative. The name had come to her in the depth of her recent fears. It was Haim, the Hebrew word for life. And he would take the old family name of Herschell.

---

[3] Obadiah 1:17

[4] Psalms 50:15

Haim Herschell had a long way to go before he would adopt for himself the English name of Ridley, but for now the whole family had yet another pressing, though not life-threatening problem, the circumcision. The problem was that no Jewish religious service could be held without the presence of at least ten male adults. Young Haim would be eight days old on Passover Eve, 14th Nissan in the Jewish year 5567. Ghetal says, "The feast of circumcision was held on the appointed day, which was the Sabbath preceding the Passover, in the month Nisan of 5567 A.M."

But right now there were hardly ten Jews left in the town, let alone ten male adults, and the father was still missing.

Then, "almost by a miracle," relates one of her sons, "he arrived at home on the seventh day after the child's birth," They thanked God for a safe return, they thanked him for the child and for the mother's life. But the ceremony, would God allow them to celebrate according to the Torah and tradition? The town was down to its last four Jewish families. Could they really find ten adult males among them? The Rabbi called on the four families. No, they couldn't. There were just not enough men in the town.

Now the pressure was on for Judah. Would God really bring them so far and not allow little Haim to enter into the Lord's covenant on the eighth day? He sent out to the neighbouring villages. They pleaded, they cajoled, they even threatened. But the people were scared. Hadn't Judah of Strzelno's own house been attacked by canon fire? And he wanted them to travel twenty miles in the ice and snow because his own neighbours had run away! Did he really expect them to risk their lives among the goyishe soldiers?

"Anyway", said one bar-room scholar, "It's not a sacrament, the child will still be a Jew! Go on home".

But the men were found. God provided for Haim, as he would for the next fifty-seven years. Haim Herschell was circumcised on the eighth day. He was a covenanted Jew, and would remain so for the rest of his life.

Chapter 3

Speak to the Israelites and say to them: 'When you enter the land I am going to give you, the land itself must observe a sabbath to the Lord.
The Bible, Leviticus 25:2

One of the most attractive and moving features of the annual Passover meal is the cup of wine left on the table for the prophet Elijah who is expected to return at that time of year. Every Jewish household hopes the prophet might honour them with his first earthly call, and so at one point in the evening a child is sent to open the front door to see if he has actually returned to their home to herald the long awaited Messiah. This was, and still is, a very real hope and many years later a granddaughter of Judah and Ghetal would write: "A younger brother of my father states that this anticipation was so present to their thoughts, that whenever in his childhood he observed a venerable and distinguished looking stranger in the streets of the town, he asked himself with awe, "Can this be Elijah?""

Sadly not everything was so good and joyful in a world where Passover often came at the same time as Easter, which was a time particularly dreaded by Polish Jews. At this time, and for many years to come, the amazing story would be revived that the Jews made use of the blood of Christian children in their Passover services. It became known as the blood libel and may have started in eastern England where a story circulated in the year 1144 that Jews had kidnapped a Christian child and drained its blood to mix with the unleavened bread of Passover. To add to the horror of this entirely untrue story the child became know as Saint William of Norwich, the city in which the story began, and was duly venerated. The imaginary martyr then became the reason for untold violence against Jewish people for hundreds of years to come.

One form of retaliation for this so-called crime of the Jews was to forcibly "convert" Jewish children to Christianity. They believed this could be done simply by baptising them against the will of their parents. Very few families remained untouched by these lies and retaliations and the Herschells themselves had been affected in a particularly tragic way.

A cousin of Haim was sent as a little girl to learn needlework at the local convent[5]. It seemed like a good idea and the nuns were very willing to share their skills with the family. But one day, either maliciously or for insanely misguided reasons, they persuaded the child to be baptised. From that day on the Church claimed her as a "Christian" and would not allow her to return to her parents. She would never again open the door to greet Elijah, or claim the Passover prize for finding the piece of matzo her father had hidden.

It is almost impossible to imagine their feelings as they watched helplessly every day, threatened by further and worse retaliations, too terrified to claim her back, as she walked the streets of the town, always accompanied by two people, her dark eyes looking for a dimly remembered family. The kindly Rabbi Hillel always spoke gently of her as *die Unglückliche*, the unfortunate one, which was, ironically, the name Adolph Hitler would use against the entire Jewish nation, *Die Juden sind Unser Unglück*,[6] the Jews are our misfortune.

But life went on, somehow, against all the odds, as it always did for Jewish families in good times and bad, and the hospitality offered to Elijah at the family's Passover Seder was also a symbol of Jewish hospitality in general and the Herschells (for it was by now a legal requirement to have a regular surname) were no exception to this. Every Sabbath twenty or thirty Jewish students or other needy people might find themselves seated at the Herschell's great dinner table to share in their Shabbat meal. The possibility of entertaining angels went back a long way. Ghetal would light the candles and for a moment, in the warmth of their protective light, the hatred of the world was held at bay. The blessing was recited:

Baruch atah Adonai, Ehlohaynu melech Ha'olam…

---

[5] Probably the order of Norbertine nuns who had settled in Strzelno in the second half of the 12th century.

[6] Quoting Heinrich von Treitschke (1834-1896)

Blessed are you Lord our God, ruler of the world, who sanctified us through His commandments and commanded us, to kindle the lights of the Sabbath.

Many local people would benefit from the prosperity of the Herschell family and the children were often sent out with gifts to poorer families, especially on the eve of the Sabbath or the great Jewish feasts. This was not only a religious duty but a sincere response to the teaching and example of Grandfather Hillel who possessed, according to one of his great-granddaughters, "that earnest faith and simplicity of character which are said to be disappearing along with many of the almost oriental customs of those days."

This was the happy, bustling, noisy, tragic Jewish world young Haim had entered and would remain in for his first eleven years. It was a truly religious world, a family world of three generations living by the Torah, the five Biblical books of Moses, Genesis to Deuteronomy.

Of course there were plenty of arguments, and endless debates, especially about the religious education of the boys in the family. Grandfather Hillel, along with Ghetal and the newly acquired Rabbi Cohen who had married Haim's older sister Miriam, would have preferred a more traditional religious training. But the more worldly Judah, though remaining what we would now call orthodox, wanted his sons to have a more liberal education and be able to take over from him in the family business.

Looking back, many years later, from his home in London Haim would say: "Having been favoured by God with pious parents, their great care was to impress my mind from childhood with a profound reverence for God, and for the Holy Scriptures."

And that reverence for God was leading the third son of Judah of Strzelno in directions nobody could have believed or expected.

As time went on it became clear to everybody that Haim was not going into the brewing business. He had developed a gift for languages and his knowledge of the scriptures grew daily. It looked as if Grandfather Hillel was going to get his wish. Haim Herschell wanted to be a Rabbi.

Chapter 4

The true sign of intelligence is not knowledge but imagination.

Albert Einstein (1879-1955)

1818, three years after Napoleon's final defeat at Waterloo, saw the first major change in the life of the young Haim Herschell. At the age of eleven he wrote a note to his mother, left the family home and set out on foot for an undisclosed destination in Russian Poland, to find a Rabbinical school. In Poland that meant a yeshiva, literally a "sitting place" where young dedicated Jewish men would study, usually to obtain *semikhah*, that is to be ordained as traditional Rabbis. The newly fashionable Western ideas about "Rabbinical seminaries" turning out modern progressive Rabbis with a broad education to meet the needs of the nineteenth century hadn't reached Poland, or Russia. If they ever did, they were rejected out of hand by the conservative Rabbis.

At the yeshiva Haim would study the Talmud, the book of Jewish civil and religious law derived from the oral traditions of the Mishnah and the five books of Moses. Like the other young men he would study day and night, often not resting or even sleeping except on the Sabbath. During the two years Haim laboured at the yeshiva he seems to have endeared himself to the Rabbi in charge and the people of the town. His daughter Ghetal tells of his announcement on his arrival that he would become a teacher in order to support himself.

Being asked what he could teach, he boldly and unhesitatingly replied: "Three languages Hebrew, German, and Polish!" If his later mastery of English is anything to go by, this little boy really was fluent in these languages as well as Yiddish, the everyday language of most Jewish people at that time, and he was duly taken on as tutor to two even smaller children.

Haim spent two years under the roof of a caring family which turned out to be distantly related to his mother and, as his daughter would write: "…at the end of which time he returned home, "not a little proud," as he has since declared, of his learning, and very strict in his religious observances."

Being "strict in his religious observances" was to be a burden as well as a strength to Haim in the years to come. But the thought of breaking from tradition was a very long way from his thoughts as he returned home to Strzelno. In fact tradition in the form of the Cabbalah, the ancient Jewish mysticism, would be his new study. By 1821, still aged only fourteen, Haim was on the move again, this time over a hundred miles away to seek new and more esoteric knowledge.

Encouraged by his mother and grandfather, not to mention his brother-in-law Rabbi Cohen, Haim was off to Piótrkow Trybunalski, the former home of Grandfather Hillel, to be instructed by Rabbi Aaron, a relative of the family and, apparently, a very devout man. "Rabbi Aaron", writes daughter Ghetal: "belonged to the Jewish sect of the Chasidim, who were not satisfied with the ordinary interpretations of Scripture, but, in addition to these, seek and find in every picture, in every story, a symbolical, allegorical, or Cabbalistical meaning, and who in this way spiritualise the whole Bible!"

Rabbi Aaron was a renowned teacher of the Cabbalah, which means "received" in Hebrew, and Haim himself would later describe it this way in his magazine *Voice of Israel*:

'The Cabbalah is a part of the oral tradition revealed, as the Jews believe, to Adam or Moses, supplementary to the written Word. The Cabbalists declare, that "the plain literal sense in the Scripture is a mere covering, under which the true sense lies hid to the profane;" that in every word of the Scriptures "seemingly superfluous to the profane, a deep mystery lies concealed, to which the Cabbalah affords the key;" that "every sentence, word, letter, and accent bears a mysterious sense." Thus the Cabbalist, by means of transpositions of letters and words, can find almost any meaning he pleases in the Scriptures.'[7]

On his return from Piótrkow Trybunalski after two years study, Haim at last started working at his father's brewery. The family business had been in

---

[7] *Voice of Israel*, vol. i. p. 155.

trouble in recent times, possibly as a result of bad debts, and all the boys were now obliged to go out to work. Very often Gentile traders in Poland at that time felt no obligation to honour debts to Jewish businessmen if it didn't suit them and Judah may have been a victim of this common practice.

But Haim wasn't cut out for the world of trade and commerce, and by now, after two years with his "mystical friend" Rabbi Aaron, he didn't even seem cut out for the religious life either. His loving and protective mother had described him as "very young, and peculiarly susceptible to every impression". So when he became friends with a young Jewish student recently returned from the decadent Prussian capital of Berlin all sides in the family expected the worst. And, for them, the worst was about to happen. Haim wanted to study in Berlin. Not the Talmud, not business, but German literature. "Unheard of! Impossible!" He would come under the "profaning influence of secular knowledge;" said his grandfather, and be lost forever.

But Haim was convinced he could support himself in his studies and business was getting so bad for Judah he had to let him go. So in 1822, still only fifteen years old, Haim set off for Germany. The farewells were long and tearful. He was leaving the country of his birth and he would only return once more. Haim Herschell would never see his beloved mother again.

Chapter 5

What is love? 'tis not hereafter;
Present mirth hath present laughter;
What's to come is still unsure:
In delay there lies no plenty,
Then come kiss me, Sweet-and-twenty,
Youth's a stuff will not endure.
William Shakespeare, *Twelfth Night*

The Royal Frederick William University, now the Humboldt University on Unter den Linden, opened its doors to students in 1810 following a brief military occupation of Berlin by Napoleon from 1806 to 1808. Berlin University was originally the Palace of Prince Heinrich of Prussia. Along with other great public buildings which still stand today, the Armoury, the State Opera House and the Old Library, not to mention the imposing Brandenburg Gate with its statue of Victory in her chariot drawn by four horses, helped establish the city of Berlin as a great centre of learning and culture.

This at least was the seat of learning daughter Ghetal saw many years later as her father's Alma Mater. But even Ghetal, who is rarely lost for words, can only recall in her Memoir: "Of the three or four years which, by his own energetic industry, he was able to spend as a student at the Berlin University, I have little to relate."

Ridley himself, though he talks about his "fellow-students", does not mention the University by name in his published testimony[8] except as the college his student friend had attended.

Berlin University had from all accounts very high standards not only for entry but for discipline and academic excellence. The philosopher Ludwig

---

[8] *Jewish Witnesses; that Jesus is the Christ.*, Edited by R. H. Herschell., 1848

Feuerbach (1804-1872) characterized it as a place where there was no duelling, no heavy drinking and, apparently, not much fun.[9] He adds: "Such striving for science, such peace and silence probably prevails nowhere like here; Other universities are like taverns compared to this workhouse."

The fact is there is no record of Haim Herschell ever registering as a student at the Royal Frederick William University in Berlin and, on the face of it; his formal education would not have qualified him for entry even in the early 19th century. Other colleges and academies had existed in Berlin since the mid-17th century and he may well have attended one of them. He clearly had acquired some serious medical knowledge and was familiar with German literature, but the records are now long gone.

Unlike Oxford and Cambridge where Jews and other dissenters were not allowed to take degrees until the 1870s Jewish undergraduates were welcomed at Berlin without any need to deny their faith.

But wherever and however he studied these were heady days for a young, inquisitive student. The influential literary works of Schiller and Goethe would take him a long way from the teaching of the reactionary Talmudic Rabbis. The world was changing fast. A great German empire was evolving and Berliners saw themselves at the centre of the world. When Haim arrived in 1822 a new high speed printing press was making Berlin the home of the mass communications industry. By the time he left for good, four years later, gas street lights were being installed on Unter den Linden and the celebrated soprano Henriette Sontag was singing at the new 1,500-seat Königstädtische Theatre on the Alexanderplatz. Felix Mendelssohn, still living at his parents' home in Leipziger Straße, was composing an Overture to Shakespeare's *A Midsummer Night's Dream*, and a lively café life was growing out of this rich cultural soil. Men of the leisured classes as well as students would eat and drink

---

[9] *"An Trinkgelagen, an Duellen, an gemeinschaftlichen Fahrten usw. ist hier gar nicht zu denken; auf keiner Universität herrscht wohl solch allgemeiner Fleiß, solcher Sinn für etwas Höheres als bloße Studentengeschichten, solches Streben nach Wissenschaft, solche Ruhe und Stille wie hier; wahre Kneipen sind andere Universitäten gegen das hiesige Arbeitshaus."*

in the bright noisy cafés, endlessly discussing art, life and business. The fashionably dressed ladies in their long flowing skirts and colourful bonnets would promenade on the wide boulevards, shopping and sharing the latest gossip. And if the social whirl within the city walls became too hectic they could always take a ride into the surrounding countryside in a comfortable horse-drawn Kremser omnibus.

But behind the gaiety and optimism lay a great unspoken fear. Untreatable and infectious diseases were a constant threat in Berlin as in every other European capital. An outbreak of cholera in 1831 would take the lives of over 1,400 Berliners as it spread with frightening speed from Russia and Poland. A major tragedy in a city of only 200,000 people.

Haim's apparent decision to switch to the study of medicine may have been influenced by these terrors and the general condition of the poor in those early days of the Industrial Revolution. Whatever his final qualification he would certainly make good use of his medical knowledge later among the impoverished Jewish remnant in Palestine.

Later Haim would find the memory of his time in Berlin almost too painful to talk about. He writes: "I pass over in silence several years of my life, which were devoted to the world, and the things of the world; during which time I kept up such a measure of conformity to the customs of my religion as I considered respectable and consistent; but my early convictions and impressions were faded and forgotten."[10]

What we do know is that Haim experienced what he describes as "an entire change in my habits and mode of life." He loved to dance and to socialise and enjoyed the friendship of free-thinking Gentile and Jewish students who considered themselves to be *aufgeklärten* (enlightened), although they sometimes found Haim's wavering religious convictions and high moral standards decidedly *alt modisch* (old-fashioned). But away from the influence of his mother and grandfather Herschell gradually fell into doubt, and eventually despair. The only thing that reminded him of his religious roots was, he says:

---

[10] *Jewish Witnesses; that Jesus is the Christ.*, Edited by R. H. Herschell., 1848

"…the little children in the streets calling after me, "Jew, Jew." Then, indeed, I realized that I belonged to the people who have become a proverb and a byeword among the Gentiles."[11]

Anti-Semitism in all its vicious forms had been a way of life back in Poland. But even there the pogroms in which many thousands of Jews would be slaughtered were still a long way off. And Hitler's *endlosen*, his final solution to the so-called Jewish problem, would not begin for another hundred years. But the seeds were being sown. Here in 1820s Berlin it usually took more subtle forms or came from the lips of children who had heard it from their indiscreet parents. Old habits died hard here, and the family of the composer Mendelssohn, who would have been Herschell's contemporary at Berlin University, like many other Jewish families found it convenient to have their son baptised a Protestant Christian at his birth.

But for the moment anti-Semitism was out of fashion, *alt modisch*, and Haim shared his life of religious indifference with students of Christian backgrounds as if both faiths were of very little importance in their brave new world. "I lived like a Christian"[12] Herschell would say, ironically echoing the bitter experience of his fellow Jews among the great majority of Catholics and Lutherans in his homeland. Rightly or wrongly, their impression of Christianity was one of hypocrisy, superstition and, more often than not, nothing less than blasphemy.

But there were good times too. It was now the summer of 1825 and like most German students Haim was planning a long vacation. A trip to England, and perhaps France, to add yet more languages to his portfolio. The only problem was how to get there with very little money. But the small matter of cost and distance would not get in the way of Haim and his group of young students with the world at their feet. They set off to walk 200 miles to the northern seaport of Hamburg where they might find casual jobs or even be able to work their passage on a ship to London. But long before they reached

---

[11] *Ibid*

[12] *Ibid*

the city Haim began to feel the burden of so many years in academic study. The yeshiva did not prepare a man for life on the road. So, footsore, tired and weary, and in spite of the determination that was already part of his character, he had to give up, and was left behind by his mocking companions.

But Herschell was to have the last laugh. When he finally reached the nearest town he made an arrangement with the driver of a waiting carriage. He could share the driver's lonely box seat and keep him company if he could only get permission from his employer to travel with them to Hamburg. This was the kind of challenge Haim preferred and was much more qualified to undertake. He had developed quite sophisticated social skills in Berlin and now they might just pay off. So he introduced himself to the passengers, one Herr von Heintz and his lady companion. Happily for our hero Herr von Heintz turned out to be both rich and generous, and took a liking to the young traveller. In fact he was so impressed with Herschell that he invited him to ride inside the carriage with him and the lady. The poor *voiturier* would travel alone after all.

Failing to see the possibility of the hand of God in any of these events Herschell continued to charm his way into the affections of the gentleman who entertained his young companion at his own expense while he remained in Hamburg, and even paid his fare to England. He also gave him letters of introduction to several acquaintances in London including the Duke of Wellington himself, along with whom he had, he said, fought at Waterloo! There is, however, no record that this letter was ever presented at No. 1 London, as the magnificent Apsley House, the Duke's London home is known. But London society would be meeting the young Polish student soon enough.

So Haim set sail for England. At sea for seven days, there would be plenty of time to brush up his language skills and speak English with his fellow travellers.

Chapter 6

When a man is tired of London he is tired of life; for
there is in London all that life can afford.

Samuel Johnson, 1777

Whatever the great city of Berlin had offered Haim it could not have prepared him for the sights and sounds of London. Sailing into the Pool among the swaying masts of a thousand trading ships from around the world, landing under the shadow of Wren's awesome domed Cathedral and the unassailable Tower, Haim must have wondered if his future didn't lie here in this, the capital of the vast British Empire. How far away little Strzelno must have seemed as he scanned the imperial skyline, taking in the quayside babble of this new language which he would one day adopt as his own.

London was home to over a million people, growing upwards and outwards to the distant suburbs. An impressive new London Bridge was being built, and beneath the Thames Isambard Kingdom Brunel was working with his father on a tunnel that would still be in use nearly two hundred years later by the London Underground railway. And before him, beyond the slippery cobbled alleys of the teaming Billingsgate fish market and the imposing new Custom House, lay the challenge he was being prepared for.

Thousands of poor Jewish immigrants, mostly from Russia and his own country of Poland, were huddled together in the bleak East End of the world's largest city. Within a few years this would become the notorious background for the works of Charles Dickens and Henry Mayhew. One day help would come from the Board of Deputies and the Jewish Board of Guardians but for now they were unrepresented, and unloved. Real emancipation would only begin a year later in 1826 when all restrictions were lifted on Jewish immigration to England.

Three years on Haim would play a part in bringing the love of his Messiah to the poor of the East End, both Jew and Gentile. But thoughts of Messiah were a long way from Herschell's mind as he discovered the delights of the London social scene further to the west. As his daughter would later report: "He entered with zest into the gaieties of a London life, his love of dancing being at that period a great temptation to him."

For nine months, according to Ghetal, he studied the language and the life of England. And he liked it. He liked it so much that he planned to return just as soon as he had completed his studies, though a less charitable source suggests he spent much more than nine months in England, which might account for his mastery of the language. [13]

By 1828 Haim had moved to Paris, perhaps to complete his now wayward education in that "city of pleasure". But, as so often happens, his plans were not God's plans. Whether it was the fog or the damp winter weather we can't know, but Haim had found himself laid up in London with a "severe illness" in the house of a Christian lady who had become not only his landlady but his nurse.

With maternal care she got him through the sickness, no mean feat at a time when life was cheap and prevention rather than cure was the only hope for most medical conditions. Real cures would not be a feature of European medicine until the 1850s. The good lady had also taken the opportunity to remove and destroy Haim's books which she often told him were "naughty books". We may never know what they were. Probably they were contemporary works of German literature, perhaps something less intellectual. But Haim found it hard to be angry with the lady who may well have saved his life and they parted as good friends. As a farewell present she gave her Jewish friend a copy of the New Testament and the address of a friend in Paris, in case he should ever need it. Predictably he threw aside the New Testament, but he kept the address and left for France.

---

[13] Morris Cerf would declare at his interrogation of 24th March 1831 that he thought Herschell had been in England "altogether for about nine years…." The Thomas Chalmers Papers, New College Library, Edinburgh University

Chapter 7

Si nous ne trouvons pas des choses agréables,
nous trouverons du moins des choses nouvelles.
(If we do not find anything pleasant,
we shall at least find something new.)
Voltaire (1694-1778)

It is hard to imagine the Eiffel Tower and the beautiful white basilica of the Sacré-Cœur not yet dominating the Parisian skyline when Haim Herschell arrived from London. In fact they would not be built in his lifetime. But he could already wander down the Avenue des Champs Elysées and across the Seine to the lively Latin Quarter. He could still have strolled round the Luxembourg Gardens and would have visited the newly built Odéon theatre close by. Making his way home he might have taken in the Sorbonne University and passed the front door of the composer Berlioz on the rue de la Harpe, where the Boulevard Saint-Michel now is.

Haim, like so many before and after him, was captivated by the French capital. It is hard for anybody not to fall in love with Paris and his daughter Ghetal writing without her usual Victorian understatement in 1869 said, "For some months he led a wild, gay life in Paris, amidst the dissipations of that city of pleasure, surrounded by companions as thoughtless as himself."

Perhaps Lady Burdon-Sanderson, as she then was, had her own memories of the City of Light as she wrote this, and was not entirely unsympathetic to her father's adventurous life.

But Paris was to be a hard mistress to the Rabbi's grandson and before long we find him down and very nearly out on the street. Haim seems to have drunk deeply from the intoxicating cup of Parisian pleasures. He had belonged, he wrote, "to that class whom the Psalmist designates 'men of the world, which have their portion in this life.'" And now that portion was running out fast.

It was at this time, in the depths of despair, poor and over seven hundred miles from home that the worst possible news came to him. Ghetal, his loving mother, had died. Haim knew the funeral would have taken place already. That was the custom, that was tradition. He wouldn't be going home. Ghetal's soul had returned to God and her earthly body would not be left to linger in the world.

The letter slipped from his hands and he cried bitterly. He knew he should have been there to say *Kaddish*, but he was here, alone in the city he would later describe as: "wholly given over to the service of sin and folly."[14]

"Yit-gadal v'yit-kadash sh'mey raba..." The ancient Aramaic words of the Mourner's Prayer came easily to the yeshiva student, "Magnified and sanctified be God's great name in the world which He has created according to His will. May He establish His kingdom soon, in our lifetime."

As he recited the familiar prayer Ghetal's last words to him returned again and again with prophetic power: "If you walk in the ways of God, we are sure to meet either in this world or in the world to come; but if you depart from the ways of God, and forget His laws, evil shall follow you even in this world, and we shall never meet - never either in this world or in the world to come."

He had long ago departed from the ways of God and now, in the depths of despair and grief, Haim once more became ill. What he endured at this time he says, could only be expressed in the words of the sixth Psalm:

> O Lord, rebuke me not in thine anger,
> Neither chasten me in thy hot displeasure.
> Have mercy upon me, O Lord; for I am weak:
> O Lord, heal me, for my bones are vexed.
> My soul is also sore vexed: but thou, O Lord, how long?
>
> Return, O Lord, deliver my soul:
> oh save me for thy mercies' sake.
> For in death there is no remembrance of thee:

---

[14] *A Visit to my Father Land, being notes of a journey to Syria and Palestine in 1843*, Ridley Herschell, 1856

In the grave who shall give thee thanks?
I am weary with my groaning;
all the night make I my bed to swim;
I water my couch with my tears.[15]

From his aching heart and torn conscience he called out to the God of his fathers. "I solemnly vowed" he said "to become very religious; I resolved to fast one day in every week, to repeat many prayers, and show kindness and charity to the poor. But this could not pacify my guilty conscience. The study of German literature had weakened my confidence in religious observances, had driven me from my own religion, and given me nothing in its place."[16]

Haim felt that God had forsaken him and cast him off forever: "I had no peace nor rest; but wherever I went, or however I was employed, I carried about with me a sense of misery that was intolerable. I could say with Job, 'The arrows of the Almighty are within me, the poison whereof drinketh up my spirit.'"

One morning Haim went out to buy something from a local shop. The shopkeeper, unaware of what he was doing, wrapped the article in a page from a large Bible, now ripped up for cheap wrapping paper. On his way home some unfamiliar lines caught Haim's eye and, as he idly read them, the words of Matthew 5:4 reached out to his breaking heart:

"Bienheureux ceux qui sont dans l'affliction, car ils seront consolés!"

Blessed are they that mourn: for they shall be comforted.

He read on out of curiosity:

"Blessed are the poor in spirit: for theirs is the kingdom of heaven. Blessed are they that mourn: for they shall be comforted. Blessed are the meek: for they shall inherit the earth. Blessed are they which do hunger and thirst after righteousness: for they shall be filled. Blessed are the merciful: for they shall obtain mercy. Blessed are the pure in heart: for they shall see God. Blessed are

---

[15] Psalms 6:1-6 (KJV)

[16] *Jewish Witnesses; that Jesus is the Christ.*, Edited by R. H. Herschell., 1848

the peacemakers: for they shall be called the children of God. Blessed are they which are persecuted for righteousness' sake: for theirs is the kingdom of heaven. Blessed are ye, when men shall revile you, and persecute you, and shall say all manner of evil against you falsely, for my sake."[17]

Who was this speaking? Whose words were causing his heart to be moved this way? Haim had never before read the New Testament. It had been a closed book to him, a hated book. The source of all the venom directed at his people. "Christ killers" they called them, though in Haim's family it was said that if the Jewish nation had sinned in crucifying Jesus of Nazareth, his family at least had had no share in the crime, as they never returned to Palestine after the Babylonian captivity!

But the work had begun, and Haim Herschell, still not knowing the source of the words he had read, shortly found himself flicking through the pages of the New Testament in a friend's home, only to find the very words speaking to him again. He borrowed the book and began to read it avidly. "At first", he would later tell his daughter, "I felt quite bewildered, and was so shocked by the constant recurrence of the name of Jesus, that I repeatedly cast the book away." Eventually he made the decision to read the mysterious volume from cover to cover. When he came to the twenty-third chapter of Matthew's gospel he was astonished at what he called, "the full disclosure of the nature of Pharisaism contained in it. Christ's lamentation over Jerusalem, in the concluding part affected me even to tears."

And in reading the account of the crucifixion, the meekness and love of Jesus astonished him, and the cruel hatred manifested against him by the priests and rulers in Israel excited within him a feeling of compassion and of indignation against Christ's accusers.

It was certainly a very moving story, but, as he would say many years later, "I did not as yet see any connexion between the sufferings of Jesus and my sins."

---

[17] Matthew 5:3-11 (KJV)

Then once again Haim put aside the New Testament. Fearing the loss of what little religious faith he had left, he decided he would study only Moses, the prophets and the Psalms. "I felt", he later wrote in his book *Jewish Witnesses that Jesus is the Christ*: "I had never hitherto studied the Bible with a desire to know what God therein taught me as an individual; to learn what He would have me think, and feel, and do".

Soon his thoughts turned once more to that book, the New Testament. "I could not get rid of the light I had acquired from it." It seemed to shed for him a radiance on every line of the Torah which he was now studying; making things clear which were before dark and mysterious to the yeshiva student; "giving order and consistency to what had formerly appeared arbitrary and unconnected .. . . ."

Haim decided, once and for all to give the dreaded book a fair hearing. After all, he reasoned, this Jesus of Nazareth came to Jews, to people who must have had the same difficulties and the same prejudices as himself. So he resolved to give the question of the truth of Christianity "a fair and a patient investigation". And he did just that. Haim applied all the skills of scholarship he had acquired to the work, and he did not find it wanting. Like so many before him, and so many to come, he found: "The more I examined into the truth of Christianity the more did the question appear to be narrowed into a small compass: Jesus of Nazareth was either the promised Messiah, or an impostor and deceiver..."

Finally he made a decision. He declared the New Testament to be: "...either a revelation from God, or an invention of lying and wicked men. After mature deliberation, I was forced to come to the conclusion that Jesus is the Messiah, and that the New Testament is, equally with the Old, the Word of God."

But this amazing conviction did not immediately bring Haim the peace he so desperately sought and expected. In fact he became more and more troubled. His heart withdrew from what his mind said was true. He was a Jew! What was he doing? What would his mother have said? What would Rabbi Hillel say? Was he to become just another "unfortunate one" like the little girl in Strzelno?

The lights of the big city were fading. The gaiety that Offenbach would immortalise in *La Vie Parisienne* drifted away like the sickly gaslight peering dimly through the Parisian fog. The joyful songs of hope faded and Paris, the fickle-hearted lover of the rich and foolish, became just another lonely town.

Walking aimlessly down the Champs Elysées one day, cold, hungry, friendless and all but homeless Haim decided to return to his miserable lodgings close by to find something to sell for food. Hopelessly he searched every corner, every grubby shelf and cupboard. Like the search for leaven on Passover eve, he examined every inch of the room, and found nothing. Nothing, that is, but an old, long forgotten letter, left perhaps like a small crumb of bread, to be found by the father as darkness fell on Passover Eve. An introduction, already fading and torn, given to him by his Christian landlady back in London.

The brief letter was addressed to the mistress of a boarding-house in Paris, and since Haim hadn't eaten all day and didn't have a lot to lose, he set out across the city in search of this last small hope. When he finally reached the address the *patronne* received him politely, and began almost immediately to talk about the subject of religion.

At this point a number of interesting characters enter the plot, some less than enthusiastic about Haim's interest in Christianity and some with serious doubts about his sincerity. Ghetal, needless to say, has no doubts about her father and presents the story as a neat and fairly seamless journey to faith. But Haim had been living on his wits for several years, His father had fallen on hard times and could no longer be relied on for funds, and there was no social security but the workhouse. He could always earn a crust by teaching, he was a natural linguist and a good teacher, but Herschell had discovered another skill in recent years. He was very attractive to ladies of a certain class and income. Not for any particular good looks or manly physique it must be said, and certainly not for his wealth or worldly prospects. But Haim Herschell was a charmer, a *roué*, attractive both to men and women for his wit and conversation, but particularly to the ladies.

As he entered that Parisian boarding-house he may just have seen the Christian ladies as marriage prospects as much as guides and mentors in his

Christian journey. Whatever the motivation Haim presented his letter of introduction and was welcomed as an enquirer into the Christian faith.

After the formal introductions and a few questions about the current state of his religion she goes on to speak of the joy and gladness of heart experienced by a believer in Jesus. Joy and gladness! This was the very thing Haim had been longing for and, according to Ghetal, he poured out his soul to her as her simple words moved him to tears of happiness.

She invited him to dinner that day, and he met people whose conversation was a great comfort and help to him. He returned that evening to his lodgings "thankful and refreshed." But his search for peace was not quite over.

Chapter 8

I look upon the Church as the only Jewish institution remaining - I know no other... If it were not for the Church, I don't see why the Jews should be known. The Church was founded by Jews, and has been faithful to its origin. It secures their history, and keeps alive the memory of its public characters, and has diffused its poetry throughout the world. The Jews owe everything to the Church...The history of the Jews is development or it is nothing.

Benjamin Disraeli (1804-1881)

The Roman Catholic Church has welcomed many Jewish believers over the centuries, some more willingly than others perhaps. But most would be quite content with the rites and rituals of Rome, much closer to Judaism in dignity and style of worship than either might have admitted. And many would even rise high in the ranks of the clergy, such as Cardinal Jean-Marie Lustiger, the Archbishop of Paris in our own time[18]. But the "repetition of Ave Marias and Our Fathers" only reminded Haim of his grandmother's remedy for all evils temporal and spiritual - the frequent repetition of the twenty-third Psalm!

Haim would not find it in his heart to be baptised in France, this Roman Catholic country which once boasted the title "First Daughter of the Church." But he had made contact with a number of Catholic clergy, one of whom, an archbishop no less, gave him a crucifix which he promptly, and rather unkindly, threw in the River Seine. To Haim it was, understandably, a *Nehushtan* - like the unholy brass serpent made by Moses in the desert and treated as an idol by the people of Israel.

He also befriended a Jewish lay Jesuit, who was secretary and librarian to the Duke of Bordeaux,[19] from whom he would learn much about Christianity. Haim would retain some affection for the Roman Catholic Church throughout

---

[18] Born Aaron Lustiger of Polish parents his mother died in Auschwitz

[19] Presumably the young Henri Charles Ferdinand Marie Dieudonné, comte de Chambord (1820-1883)

his life and, even though he would be baptised in the Church of England, it would be among the so-called non-conformists that he would make his home. Meanwhile he had major financial problems to deal with.

Paris had much to offer those who could afford to enjoy her pleasures, but Haim Herschell was once again running out of funds. And to make things worse, news had got back to Poland of his conversion, or apostasy as they would call it. His father and most of the family would almost certainly disown him and there would be no more relief from that direction.

His new friends at the boarding-house had recommended him to go back to England, and he himself was keen to return there though he hardly had enough money to feed himself let alone make the journey to London.

But Haim would have to get used to the ways in which God would provide for him in future. A letter arrived from his hostess of the previous evening containing 250 francs[20], a loan, but more than enough to get him to England and find work. She also enclosed letters of introduction from some of her boarders to Christians in England, among them Hannah More, the writer and philanthropist and, it seems, the Bishop of London, or somebody very close to him.

Ridley left Paris for London at the end of 1828, feeling as if, as he would say on a return visit: "the very stones beneath me cried aloud of the mercies of our blessed and gracious God."

The winter of 1828-29 was exceptionally cold. In London there was a continuous frost from the 16th to the 24th of January and there was ice in the Thames on the 23rd. At the age of twenty-one Herschell arrived back in London, entered an Institution for Jews "inquiring into the truths of Christianity" in Somerstown, and became, after one or two incidents which we shall discover later, a model inmate. He had come home.

The Institution had been established in July 1829 by a young charismatic Polish Jew called Erasmus H. Simon. His real name was Haim Simeon, the son

---

[20] The lowest denomination banknote at the time and more than a month's wages for the average French worker

of Rabbi Abraham Simeon, but known to his friends simply as Judah. He had taken the name Erasmus, after the Dutch reformer, when he was baptised a Christian in 1820.

Erasmus had recently returned from America where he had, among other ambitious ventures, tried to establish a Hebrew Christian Church. Having failed to realise his dream in the New World he settled, with his Scottish wife Barbara in London and sought the patronage of the Bishop of London to establish a similar church in England. Surprisingly, given Erasmus's rather poor track record in America and the potential conflict with the Church of England, the Bishop seems to have been quite enthusiastic, and in a short note delivered on 22nd January 1829 he writes: "The Bishop of London presents his compliments to Mr. Simon, and requests the favour of his mentioning to him the names of any other respectable persons of his own nation who concur with him in the views which he takes of a Hebrew Christian Church."[21]

Erasmus clearly found some other "respectable persons of his own nation" but at this stage an element of confusion enters, not least as far as the good Bishop is concerned. In her *Memoir of Erasmus*[22] his wife switches easily between the ideas of a Hebrew church and a less ambitious "institute" for enquirers. This ambiguity may have been intentional on Erasmus's part in order to gain support for the institute which was to secretly incorporate the new church itself, like some ecclesiastical cuckoo's egg. But Erasmus had apparently made it clear to the Bishop: "All that we desire," he wrote following a brief interview early in 1829, "is that you would not consider us as dissenters, but countenance us in reviving our ancient claim of having our own National Church as Hebrews.[23]

Simon saw this as nothing less than the revival of the "Hebrew Church at Jerusalem, of which the apostle James was the bishop."

---

[21] *Memoir of Erasmus H. Simon,*, Barbara A. Simon, 1837

[22] *Ibid*

[23] *Ibid*

The Bishop, Charles James Blomfield,[24] was a very tolerant and kindly man and may have seen this as nothing more than another movement within the broad Church of England.[25] It was not for nothing the Church of England was known as the *via media*, the middle way, which embraced, and still embraces, all shades of Christianity from Anglo-Catholic to Evangelical and beyond. He may well have negotiated a deal with Simon[26] but, whatever the actual process, within five months a committee of Anglican worthies had been formed under the Bishop of London called the Friends of the Hebrew Nation, and Erasmus opened the doors of number nine Randolph Street to enquirers after *Yeshua Ha Mashiach*, Jesus the Messiah.

Twenty-two inmates, including Ridley Herschell, initially entered the institute. Twelve would be baptised a year later. Ten members, ten adult males, including Ridley, were eventually to form the basis of the new "National church of Jews who believe." They would surely be needing their own bishop soon, thought Erasmus as his motley crew settled down to their new communal life.

Ridley found the life and teaching amenable but the "spiritual rest" offered by the Christian ladies in the Parisian boarding house still eluded him. One day, in despair Haim threw himself down on the ground, begging the Lord to give him peace.

Suddenly these words of Jesus came into his mind,

'Hitherto have ye asked nothing in my name.'[27]

"I cannot describe the reluctance I felt to pray in the name of Jesus," said Herschell, "and yet I saw how inconsistent was this reluctance with the belief that he is the Saviour of the world." [28]

Haim would never forget the struggle of that moment. At length he was

---

[24] 1786-1857

[25] Just as Messianic Jewish services are held in the Anglican church in Jerusalem today

[26] Inmates were required to worship regularly at Somers' Chapel, Seymour Street, Somerstown

[27] John 16:24 (KJV)

[28] *Jewish Witnesses; that Jesus is the Christ.*, Edited by R. H. Herschell., 1848

enabled to cry out: "Lord, I believe that Jesus is the Messiah, the Redeemer, and King of Israel, who was wounded for our transgressions, and bruised for our iniquities; for His sake have mercy upon me, and give me peace."[29] He continues: "No sooner had I offered this prayer than my burden was removed; the peace of God, that passeth all understanding, entered into my soul. I felt that I was redeemed from destruction, that God loved me, that Christ had died for me, and washed me from all my sins in his own blood".

There was no way back, Haim Herschell had been reborn.

---

[29] *Ibid*

Chapter 9

At three, I started Hebrew school. At ten, I learned a trade.
I hear they've picked a bride for me. I hope she's pretty.
From Tradition, *(Fiddler on the Roof)*, Sheldon Harnick

Helen Skirving Mowbray, born 17th August 1797, had been living with her grandfather when her mother, Helen Pillans, died in 1813. At the age of sixteen she had been called home to the Scottish seaport of Leith near Edinburgh to supervise her father's household. William, her father, was a successful merchant in the town and Helen was his eldest child.

"It was a marvel to many", her daughter's memoir records, "that she could find time for pursuing her music and drawing without neglecting her duty to her father's family. But her mind was equally capable of being directed to great and small things; and though she spent hours in painting, and arranged the music for weekly concerts, in which she at that time took part, she did not neglect the most minute detail of household management."[30]

Helen's scholarly achievements won her an entry in Frederic Boase's respected *Modern English Biography* which contains over 25,000 biographies of notable English, and presumably Scottish, men and women from 1850 to 1916.

By the age of about twenty-five she had already lost four members of her family to the scourge of consumption, and her thoughts had turned, after the death of one of her brothers, to more spiritual matters. She became a committed Christian and, in the words of one admirer, "experienced that change of heart, which the Scriptures tell us must take place in every one before they can become a child of God."[31]

---

[30] *Far above Rubies, Memoirs of H. S. H., by her Daughter.* Edited by R. H. Herschell, 1854

[31] *Ibid*

Much of her time seems to have been spent writing to younger brothers and sisters as well as wayward cousins and other relatives about the state of their souls or their moral condition. The fire of her earlier conversion was still blazing and she would address them in these rather bossy but sincere terms: "As eldest of my father's family, I have always considered it my duty to address my younger brothers and sisters, on the most important of all subjects, as soon as I thought them old enough to receive such instruction."[32]

and,

"Although it is generally considered as absurd to talk to a young man about religion, as it would be to talk to a young lady of mathematics or algebra, yet I intend to avail myself of those privileges which our near relationship affords me, to commit this absurdity, if it be one."[33]

and the wonderfully dismissive line,

"Religion, I doubt not, is a subject on which you have bestowed little of your attention."[34]

Now at thirty-two she had a contented life and, relieved of much responsibility since her father's remarriage, Helen settled into a world of study and pursued the many subjects that interested her. From the comfortable family home at 5 Hope Street[35] in Leith she seems to have moved easily in the middle class society of Edinburgh and even on the fringes of high society in London. In 1828 she wrote: "On Monday I spent a delightful day with the author of the Cry from the Desert,[36] and his wife. They are a most interesting couple, of much spiritual discernment, and seem to live habitually under the influence of those glorious hopes which should animate all those who are 'waiting for the coming of the Lord.'"[37]

---

[32] *Ibid*

[33] *Ibid*

[34] *Ibid*

[35] Now Casselbank Street at the bottom of Leith Walk about a mile from Edinburgh city centre.

[36] *A Cry from the Desert*, *"Behold the Bridegroom cometh."*, a popular tract published in London in 1827

[37] *Far above Rubies, Memoirs of H. S. H., by her Daughter.* Edited by R. H. Herschell, 1854

This was the comfortable world of Helen Skirving Mowbray, age thirty-two, spinster of the parish of Leith. Her marriage prospects had been willingly sacrificed to the needs of her family and she was content with her lot. Her Christian faith grew and matured daily as she studied the scriptures and the Hebrew language. In February 1827 she wrote to a friend: "I may mention to you (but it is quite *entre nous*), that I have been taking lessons in Hebrew, and can now read it with tolerable fluency. . . I am sure such a study, where it interferes not with duty, is approved of God, and tends to edification."[38]

In time she found herself and her sympathies being directed more and more "to the promises held out to His chosen people Israel."[39]

It was about this time that Helen came under the influence of a charismatic Church of Scotland minister called Edward Irving. Mr Irving's key themes were the imminent restoration of Israel and the Second Coming of Jesus. He even set a date for the Messiah's return, 1864!

In 1822 the thirty-year-old Irving had been called to London to preach at the Caledonian chapel, but the congregation grew so fast that in 1824 a new and larger church had to be built for him in Regent Square, London.

"He has turned religion and the Caledonian Chapel topsy-turvy", wrote the contemporary essayist William Hazlitt. "He has held a play-book in one hand and a Bible in the other, and quoted Shakespeare and Melancthon in the same breath."[40]

Irving was certainly a showman, and everybody loved a free show. Rich and poor, high and low flocked to see the big Calvinist preacher tear into the great and the good of the day. Nobody was so high or so powerful that Irving could not bring them down. But still they flocked to hear him.

While Edward Irving preached to his uptown audience in West London, Haim Herschell had settled into the routine of the Institution in the much less

---

[38] *Ibid*

[39] *Ibid*

[40] *The Spirit of the Age*, William Hazlitt, 1824

fashionable Somerstown. Mr Erasmus Simon, the Superintendent, was said to be "much pleased" with Herschell's modest and humble demeanour, and with his "candid acknowledgment that he needed to enter on a new course of life." On 14th of April 1830, twelve of the inmates were baptised at St. James' Church Westminster, now St. James', Piccadilly, by the Bishop of London. Haim Herschell was one of them. His sponsors were Oliver Farrer, Oliver's sister Mary[41] and her husband the Rev. Henry Colborne Ridley BD, Rector of Hambledon in Buckinghamshire, whose name he took in addition to his own.

Shortly after his baptism Herschell travelled to Clifton, near Bristol, to present his letter of introduction from Paris to the eighty-five year old Hannah More. Miss More apparently took a great interest in him and introduced him in turn to many other eminent Christians in Bristol, including the writer and anti-slavery campaigner Mary Anne Schimmelpennick.

These skirmishes among the rich and famous would soon bring Ridley into contact with that very same Edward Irving who had so impressed Helen Mowbray. And within these tightly knit circles of English and Scottish society it seems his recent baptism sponsor, Mrs Ridley, was also a very good friend of Miss Helen Mowbray.

---

[41] Ghetal refers to her as Miss Farrer in the *Memoir* but she had married Henry Colborne Ridley in 1808

Chapter 10

I cannot convert men; I can only proclaim the Gospel.

Dwight Lyman Moody (1837-1899)

Death is no respecter of class, or indeed nobility, and when King George III's favourite daughter Amelia died in 1810 at the age of twenty-seven it probably pushed his ailing mind over the edge into insanity. The next year his adulterous, extravagant and idle son George, Prince of Wales, became Prince Regent until the death of his father in 1820. By the time of his own death in 1830, as George IV, England had changed beyond recognition. The Industrial Revolution was bringing immense wealth to a small number of people but the streets of London were filled with poverty and disease. Fear of a real revolution like the ones in France and America had been ever present.

King George IV, debauched and addicted to alcohol and laudanum, had certainly left the country some fine Regency art and architecture, but he had also bequeathed his people a hedonistic and immoral lifestyle.

In 1830, this was the world into which Ridley Haim Herschell was called to bring the light of the Gospel, and like St. Paul himself had said, it would be "to the Jew first, and also to the Greek."[42]

By now life among the fleshpots of Bristol was taking its toll. "I felt", he said, "conscience smitten at the course I was pursuing" and he longed to return to "making known the truths of Christianity to my own people." In spite of tempting offers of ordination following his baptism and the prospect of a comfortable living in the Church of England Ridley yearned to be back working among his kinsmen in the East End. He would leave Bristol and return to London.

Meanwhile, news of his baptism had reached Poland. The response was

---

[42] Romans 1:16

harsh and predictable: "Thy name shall henceforth be blotted out and no more named by us", wrote one member of the family, "may the hottest judgments of the Almighty fall upon thee, because thou hast forsaken the God of Israel; and joined thyself to idols."[43]

Not only had Haim been disowned by his family, he was now under constant threat of violence from his former Jewish friends and companions in London. One even went so far as to carry a gun with the intention of shooting him if he got the chance.

Such an extreme response was brought on by a deep conviction that Christians worshipped more than one God. The Sh'ma, the prayer that even the least observant Jew is expected to know and to say daily, says:

Sh'ma Yisrael Adonai eloheinu Adonai echad... "Hear O Israel, the Lord our God, the Lord is One. Blessed be His name, whose glorious kingdom is forever and ever."

The difficult Christian doctrine of one Trinitarian God, the Holy Trinity, is often explained in terms of ice, water and steam being the same thing in substance, or three pairs of hands linked in an eternal circle. But even though the idea of one God, Father, Son and Holy Spirit remains a difficult subject, Ridley would have found that the Nicene Creed of the Church, a summary of its fundamental, unchangeable beliefs, drawn from the Church's deep Jewish roots, is in complete agreement with the Sh'ma...

> We believe in one God,
> The Father, the almighty,
> maker of heaven and earth,
> of all that is,
> seen and unseen...

On his return to Somerstown Herschell and others started to hold nightly meetings after work at a room in the East End of London. Union Street,

---

[43] *Jewish Witnesses; that Jesus is the Christ.*, Edited by R. H. Herschell., 1848

Bishopsgate, now Brushfield Street was close to where the Liverpool Street railway terminus would be built in 1872. But for now it was a dark and dangerous place for a young, zealous Christian convert.

One night Ridley had announced that he would be explaining to the meeting why he had become a Christian and invited the mainly Jewish residents to join them. This did not go down well in an area whose main attraction was Dirty Dick's pub and whose residents were, on the whole, what Herschell himself called Jews "of the baser sort." In other words they didn't need much excuse to start a riot. And that's exactly what happened. Uproar followed his introduction and, as the audience threw chairs and any other missiles they could lay their hands on, he made his undignified escape through the roof, down the back stairs and into a passing butcher's cart. Shaken but not injured, and liberally spattered with mud by the backup rabble waiting outside the house the evangelist made his way home to Somerstown. The Shillibeer Omnibus service that ran between the City and the suburbs of Paddington and Regent's Park, passed close to the Institute but Ridley probably walked and reflected.

Clearly, bringing the Gospel to the good people of Whitechapel was not going to be easy. And to add to the troubles of the one-time yeshiva student, he was summoned before the magistrates for holding a disorderly meeting. The charge was eventually dismissed, and the services were allowed to go on, with the preacher being accompanied by an officer in uniform. But even with this military presence, Ridley was never allowed to speak without constant interruption from his audience.

Undaunted, and full of zeal for the work, the next ambitious project, under the leadership of the indefatigable Mr Simon was to form that Jewish-Christian Church with a Jewish bishop and an all-Jewish congregation. Given the age and financial situation of the would-be founders, their plans looked set for certain failure. But they were to find unexpected support among the followers of the now famous Edward Irving, the so-called Irvingites. Irving's followers, many of whom were wealthy, were constantly looking for signs of the end times and were convinced that any movement among Jews to unite as followers of Jesus was a sure sign the restoration of Israel and the return of

Messiah was at hand! Their financial support was certainly seen as providential by the impoverished group.

On the evening of 14th February 1831, just eighteen months after the opening of the Institute, the reconstituted Hebrew Church, including its bishop Aaron Levita, Secretary Elias Lebenheim, three elders, one of whom was Ridley Herschell, and several deacons, was unilaterally declared open. Erasmus himself does not seem to have held an elected office, unless he was a humble unrecorded deacon, but given his tendency to compare himself to Moses when the going got tough, it is likely he saw himself as above and beyond this democratic process. Oblivious to the Apostle's teaching that "t There is neither Jew nor Greek, slave nor free, male nor female, for you are all one in Christ Jesus."[44] Erasmus wrote to the Bishop of London three days later with the enthusiasm and disrespect of the true fanatic: "My Lord, when I had last the pleasure of seeing your Lordship, the interview was too short, and your Lordship's mind not sufficiently prepared for more than the disclosure which I at that time made; but, as it is as much my principle as my disposition to be perfectly candid with your Lordship, I now (since you prefer it in writing) proceed briefly to inform your Lordship of the re-constitution of the Apostolic Hebrew Church on the primitive model of our Hebrew church government, and in perfect conformity with the faith once delivered to the saints; which conformity involves our unity of faith and charity with the Church of England, as an Apostolic Gentile Church."[45]

The response was swift and the Bishop was not pleased. "Nothing could exceed the surprise and displeasure of the Committee, who were at that time all members of the Established Church", writes Barbara Simon, "except the astonishment of Erasmus that there should have been any misapprehension of his intentions."[46]

The Bishop's letter to the Secretary of the Society is reproduced here in

---

[44] Galatians 3:28

[45] 1st Report of the Operative Jewish Converts Institution incorporating the 2nd Annual Report of the Friends of the Hebrew Nation prior to their incorporation, Bodleian Library, Oxford.

[46] *Memoir of Erasmus H. Simon,*, Barbara A. Simon, 1837

full from the 2nd Annual Report of the Friends of the Hebrew Nation:

Sir,

It is with sincere regret that I communicate to you my intention of resigning the office of Patron of the Society of Friends of the Hebrew Nation, and of withdrawing my name from the list of its members. The notions which Mr. Simon now professes to hold, respecting the Jewish and Christian Sabbath, are so different from what I understood him to entertain when I first conversed with him on the subject; and his views with respect to the formation of an independent Hebrew Christian church in this kingdom, with its own Bishop, and its own peculiar rites, are so wild, that I can no longer, consistently with my duty to the Church of England, directly or indirectly sanction the Institution over which he presides. I give him full credit for piety and sincerity of purpose, but I can by no means concur in his opinions. I have to request that you will communicate this to the Committee, and to assure them of the pain which it has cost me to form this determination.

I have the honour to be

Your most obedient faithful servant,

C. L. London

Within days the management committee had closed ranks and invited Erasmus to resign as Superintendent, which he did. Another new society with similar but broader aims was approached and they united with them to form the new Operative Jewish Converts Institution. Erasmus was replaced in 1831, "after necessary reconstruction"[47], by the Revd, J.C. Reichardt. The whole operation was overseen by Joseph Frey's London Society for the Promotion of Christianity Amongst the Jews, known today as CMJ or the Church's Ministry Among the Jewish People and they moved to a new five acre compound within the Society's palatial headquarters at Palestine Place, Bethnal Green.

But Erasmus Simon receives no mention in this context in the lengthy

---

[47] *The History of the London Society for Promoting Christianity Amongst the Jews* from 1809 to 1908, W.T. Gidney, 1908

history of the Society published in 1908[48] and he would later find himself accused of running a private matchmaking service for eligible Jewish converts while he was in charge. A few years later the old institution's home at Randolph Street was razed to the ground, to make way for the new London Midland railway.

The residential course at the new Institute was to be for three years and would, in the words of the 23rd annual report of its management[49]:

"...furnish employment to destitute Christian Jews, in order to give spiritual instruction to its inmates, in the hope that his means of usefulness may be rather increased than diminished by such a step."

Printing and bookbinding would be the trade taught and carried on at the Institution from that time right through to the end of the Second World War, even though the Institution itself would move home a couple of times, ending its days in Bodney Road, Hackney.

Did the end justify the means for Erasmus Simon? Was his failure due to his own pride or the stubbornness of the established church? Erasmus was not, by his own admission, a team player. He was beyond doubt a leader but there were fatal weaknesses in his character.

In a last ditch stand he moved his supporters, his institute and his church, to a house in Kensington. Ridley Herschell was with them and had, it seems, become Erasmus's right hand man. They had been planning the establishment of a similar institute in Ireland, apparently without the consent of the old committee. But Erasmus may not have told Herschell that his plans were unofficial just as he hadn't been entirely open with the Bishop of London or the society he had worked for in America[50].

After sleeping on straw for several nights while they waited for furnishings

---

[48] *Ibid*

[49] CMJ

[50] The American Society for Meliorating the Condition of the Jews

to arrive they settled in and started to hold weekly meetings in the house for reading and conversation on the Scriptures. These meetings were frequently attended by Edward Irving himself and members of his congregation. And on a number of occasions, at the invitation of her friend Mrs Ridley, Miss Helen Mowbray also attended.

Chapter 11

Brief is life, but love is long.

Alfred, Lord Tennyson (1809-1892)

"Helen, Helen, come and see a Jew," shouted the young girl with gentle mockery from the window. Helen Mowbray was in London for the first time. Her companion, a young friend from Edinburgh had spotted a street trader from the window. Aware of Helen's growing love for anything and everything Jewish she had taken the opportunity to make fun of her. But Helen's interest in things Jewish was more serious than her friend could imagine.

She had learned to read Hebrew with some fluency and was now studying some of the Talmudic writings which she had sent another friend out to find among London's many book-stalls.

Soon Helen would make the acquaintance of Mr Irving of whom she had heard and admired so much, and a friendship would form that would last sporadically until his untimely death. Whenever she was in London Helen would take every opportunity to hear his lectures on the prophetic Scriptures and she entered with her usual enthusiasm into the study of prophecy as her interest and love grew for the nation whose history forms the bulk of the Scriptures, the Jewish people.

One day, on a visit with the Irvings to the house in Kensington, her friend Mrs Ridley introduced Helen to a young Polish Jew who had been making a name for himself as "the lion of the religious world of Clifton" and was now, apparently, about to establish another Jewish institution in the heart of Dublin. Ridley was by nature, if not by birth, a gentleman and it is not hard to imagine the scene as Mrs Ridley approached him, her crinoline petticoats rustling, indiscreetly playing the role of matchmaker and saying, "Mr Herschell, may I introduce Miss Helen Mowbray? Miss Mowbray, Mr Ridley Herschell."

It is nice to think that the young Herschell, formally dressed in a broad shouldered tail-coat for the evening, would have said, with just the hint of a Polish accent, "Enchanted, Mademoiselle!" and have given a slight click of his heels in the manner of a Polish army officer.

"Miss Mowbray takes a great interest in the restoration of the Jewish nation Mr Herschell, I'm sure you'll have a lot to talk about."

And it seems Ridley was indeed enchanted by Miss Mowbray and they had a great deal to talk about. And even the restraints of 19th century courtship could not have stifled the unspoken words they shared at that first meeting, even in those first brief moments.

Helen was no longer young. Her mother had died at forty and, since 1823, a girl could marry at the age of twelve without parental consent. Life could be brief. Ridley was younger but his shadowy unrecorded experiences in Berlin and Paris had familiarised him with the ways of the world. They had in their different ways both lived for the world and their glances encapsulated experiences that broke through the restraints of late Georgian manners. Their common faith had not become a substitute for living but a response to it.

Within a few weeks, on a visit to an Irvingite church in Row, Scotland,[51] they had become engaged. They were to be married in Helen's homeland when the banns had been read. But news travels fast, especially bad news, and by the time Helen had announced the happy event to her father in February 1831 he had already been made aware of Ridley's past, both real and imagined. Within days moves were being made to stop the marriage and cut off Helen's inheritance from her grandfather, James Pillans. Letters flew almost hourly between the powerful Thomas Chalmers, Professor of Divinity at the University of Edinburgh and future Moderator of the Free Church of Scotland, and Helen's stepmother, a distant relative of Chalmers[52], in an attempt to stop support among Helen's friends in Edinburgh...

---

[51] Now Rhu on the east bank of the Gareloch, 26 miles north west of Glasgow

[52] Margaret's father was also a clergyman, William Chalmers (1755-1838)

Saturday 19th March 1831

Mr Campbell might be told of the strong impression all the world entertains of Herschell's duplicity and the bogus holiness of his character as a professing Christian – that his character becomes more and more suspicious...[53]

Saturday 19th March 1831

Mr MacDonald's letter I understood having arrived on Thursday contained information of some importance – it related to some gross immoralities of which Herschell had been guilty in Paris immediately previous to his entering the London Institution – of course all this period he purported to be an enquirer into Christianity...[54]

Saturday 2nd April 1831

Miss M's announcement of her correspondence with Herschell was made to her father on the evening of Wednesday the 9th February. His impassive reply was "Helen I would sooner see you dead at my feet"[55]

Saturday 2nd April 1831

...before Miss M's recovery from measles with which she was seized that very day, her father discovered that he and the other Trustees had sufficient control over her finances.[56]

And from William Mowbray himself:

Monday 25th April 1831

I return enclosed Mr O. Farrer's letter of which I have taken a copy to

---

[53] The Thomas Chalmers Papers, New College Library, Edinburgh University

[54] *Ibid*

[55] *Ibid*

[56] *Ibid*

send to Mr Tudor and as soon as I receive anything in reply I shall give you notice. I have now received a direct promise in writing that there shall be no marriage either with Mr H. or any other person without my consent.[57]

Any hopes of a formal courtship and family wedding had been shattered, as Ghetal explains with some allusions to anti-Semitism which are really not borne out by the correspondence: "Although the fact of connecting herself with one of the despised people brought shame and reproach upon her, she was willing to bear all with cheerfulness for her Saviour's sake."[58]

Vitriolic as they sometimes are, none of the letters of her stepmother Margaret Mathison on the subject mentions the word Jew or Jewish. They really do just see Herschell as a opportunist.

As for Chalmers he seems to have welcomed the opportunity to attack the minister of the church at Row, John McLeod Campbell, who was accused of introducing the unorthodox charismatic worship of the Irvingites to his own congregation. McLeod Campbell was also at the heart of the so called Row Heresy[59] and was seen as a threat to the stability of the Scottish Church, though he denied any connection with the Irvingite Helen and Ridley.

Probably as a result of Chalmers' doubts about Campbell's honesty he would do little to support him when he was finally deposed by the General Assembly in 1832.

But McLeod Campbell was a sincere if misguided man and may well have been telling the truth. Helen and her entourage would almost certainly have been staying at the fashionable seaside resort of Helensburgh overlooking the Firth of Clyde rather than the small village of Row up on Gareloch. Campbell writes ingenuously to Chalmers to say he had once met Helen on the high road but: "…she was one of several persons passing in a carriage and a gentleman

---

57 *Ibid*

58 *Far above Rubies, Memoirs of H. S. H., by her Daughter.* Edited by R. H. Herschell, 1854

59 The Row Heresy. John McLeod Campbell attacked the High Calvinist doctrine of Predestination and argued that Jesus had offered salvation to all. He was deposed by the General Assembly but his views have now become mainstream in the church.

with me bowed to her and mentioned her name but I actually would not know her if I met her at this moment."[60]

Herschell himself now found himself under attack from all sides. If he could do anything to add to the shame of converting to Christianity, getting baptised and changing his name, it would be to marry a Gentile woman, a *shiksa*. And that's just what he was planning to do. Some in the Jewish community took every opportunity to spoil the marriage by digging up disreputable stories from Herschell's past life in London and Paris and, as a friend later wrote: "Those Jews who formerly dipped with him in the cup of this world's pleasures left no stone unturned which might effect his ruin."

Even Mr Simon's glowing reference was tainted by the allegations of his own matchmaking and made no impression on Mrs Mowbray. He writes: "Since the time that Mr Herschell entered (the institution) as an inquirer after truth, I can truly affirm that his growth in grace has been demonstrated, not in word only, but in deed . . . The docility of a dear child, the constant sense that those who have been forgiven much should love much, has marked his walk and conversation. In one word, I, as in the sight of God, believe that his whole heart and mind are bent upon following our Saviour in all things."

Indeed that is exactly what had happened to Ridley Haim Herschell. He had repented. He had once and for all turned away from his past life, however recent. And he apparently said as much to Mr Mowbray when he was interviewed by him on 18th March 1831. Mrs Mowbray reports to the Revd. Chalmers: "Mr M had an interview with him (Herschell) today at Mr Hutchinson's the result of which proved but little satisfactory. Though to most of the charges he was obliged to plead guilty – but professed repentance of them – and that all debts he had contracted were all paid for – but I must not attempt to say more on paper. When can I see you dear sir?"[61]

Three days later, 24th March 1831 a man called Morris Cerf was summoned from London to the home of the Revd. Dr. Gordon in Edinburgh

---

[60] The Thomas Chalmers Papers, New College Library, Edinburgh University

[61] *Ibid*

to be interrogated by himself, Mr and Mrs Mowbray and Mr Andrew T. Bowden.

In the resulting document[62] Ridley Herschell's character is torn apart by the professing Jewish Christian. He had, he claimed, known Ridley for many years in London and Manchester. He had known his brother, presumably Joseph, who had fallen on hard times. Ridley was, he insisted, a thoroughly bad lot. There would be no marriage in Scotland.

Sadly there seems never to have been any reconciliation with the family in Scotland either. On Thursday 29th September 1831 Ridley and Helen were married in London at St. Mary Abbots, Kensington under special licence. Erasmus and Barbara Simon were among the witnesses. She was thirty-four, he was twenty-four. There would clearly be no dowry to relieve the straitened circumstances to come. Ridley had finally married for love. "I believe God has fitted me and called me to labour among His people," wrote Helen, "and consequently in His work I shall in His own time most assuredly be engaged. I am therefore encouraged to pray earnestly for it in the face of seeming impossibilities."[63]

When her father died just two years later in May 1833 he cut her out of his will entirely except for a relatively small sum which he gave to all the surviving children of both marriages. Helen had, it seems, received £1,125 from her grandfather in spite of efforts to withhold it from her. Her father left her a further £875 to match the amount of £2,000 given to the children of his second marriage who did not benefit from the grandfather's will. This would be enough for her to live on the interest at about the level of a senior clerk in a London office. Like the clerk she could employ a maid but she would live a far less privileged life than the rest of her family.

James could not bring himself to let his eldest daughter starve but it is a measure of his bitterness at the marriage that while distributing his great wealth of land and property among his children and grandchildren he could

---

[62] *Ibid*

[63] *Far above Rubies, Memoirs of H. S. H., by her Daughter.* Edited by R. H. Herschell, 1854

record in a legal document: "...excepting always the said Helen Skirving Mowbray whom I do hereby expressly cut off and exclude from all share and interest in the succession to my property."[64]

Helen wrote from London with a hint of resignation to an old friend in Edinburgh: "You may tell all who inquire about me that I have all the happiness that this world can give me; may it never make me forget that it is indeed not my rest."

---

[64] William Mowbray's Testament, 30 August 1833, Scotland's People

Chapter 12

Preach not because you have to say something,
but because you have something to say.

Richard Whately (1787-1863)

By the 1830s, before the new steam railway had any serious effect on travel, the stagecoach, built by skilled craftsmen, gleaming with up to fifty coats of protective paint and pulled by six strong horses was in its heyday. With vastly improved roads it was possible to cover fifty miles in a day, putting Oxford within easy reach of London, and the peaceful riverside town of Henley-on-Thames a mere daytrip away.

For Mr and Mrs Herschell their visit to Henley was something more than a day out, but in the warm late summer sunshine of September 1831 it was a welcome opportunity to be alone by the river, away from the busy life in Kensington.

They had hoped to call on some friends in High Wycombe, a market town by the River Wye on the edge of the Chiltern Hills, but finding they'd gone away Ridley decided, for no apparent reason, to head for Henley.

"One recommendation was," wrote Mrs Herschell in a letter from that time, "that he knew the innkeeper and his wife to be pious people."

He also may have wanted to show his new wife the gentle Oxfordshire scenery with its quietly rolling meadows in pastel shades of green and yellow contrasting with the more rugged beauties of her Scottish homeland. But many years later they agreed that it was God's hand guiding their steps, leading them to a household which was to become almost a second home to them.

Ridley knew just two families in Henley-on-Thames, and even those, says Helen, "so slightly, that he was considering whether or not he would call upon them during our visit." But the morning after their arrival, as they were taking a stroll, they bumped into one of these very gentlemen, just a hundred yards from the inn where they were staying. Raising his top hat he warmly greeted

Ridley and his new wife like old friends and insisted they join him at the meeting of the Henley Bible Society that afternoon. And so they did. And who else should be at the meeting but the other gentlemen Ridley had met, the Revd. Mr Bolton and a friend from Reading. God was certainly moving in mysterious ways for the Herschells.

During dinner together Mr Bolton, who was an Independent clergyman, insisted Mr Herschell should preach in his chapel on Sunday evening. Ridley agreed, but Helen was nervous. Her young husband had certainly spoken confidently enough to the groups who met at the house in Kensington. He had even bravely faced angry crowds in London's grim East End. But to preach from a pulpit at a Sunday service in Henley-on-Thames, even an evening service, made her feel "a little anxious."

Helen needn't have worried. "Concerning his preaching," she later proudly wrote, "I shall only say that I fully believe it is that to which God has called him and that when he has exercised the gift for some time longer, he will be an able minister of the New Testament." And so he would be.

But it wasn't only Helen who was impressed with Ridley's sermon that evening. The lady of the local manor, Mrs Fuller-Maitland, formerly Miss Bethia Ellis, was there too. Bethia, who already owned a substantial property in Essex called Stansted Hall, had married Ebenezer Fuller-Maitland, sometime MP for Lostwithiel, Wallingford & Chipenham, and now lived nearby with him, along with most of their twelve children, at the vast family home of Park Place, Berkshire.

Even by the standards of the time Park Place was a very desirable residence among the upper classes, as well as the growing nouveau riche business class. The estate had once been owned by Frederick, Prince of Wales, the eldest son of George II, and Queen Victoria herself, presumably on a day trip from nearby Windsor Castle, would view the house when it was offered for sale in 1865.

Park Place sat, and sits to this day, amid nine hundred acres of parkland on a high plateau overlooking a broad blue horseshoe in the Thames above Henley, close to the village of Remenham. A previous owner, General Conway, following a long and distinguished military career had made many improvements to the property in the 1780s including a major tree planting and landscaping programme which gave the great white house a gem like quality set amid the green woodlands rolling gently down to one of the prettiest, and cleanest, reaches of the Thames.

The Fuller-Maitlands, who had owned the property since 1824, apart from being very well off could, one way or another, trace their line back to 1066 AD and the Norman Conquest. The Herschells on the other hand were quite poor, but could trace theirs with some confidence to the Babylonian exile of the Jews, about 600 BC, from where Ridley's family moved to Spain.

With such a pedigree, and the knowledge of Scripture to go with it, Ridley Haim Herschell was irresistible to this Christian lady with a heart for the Jewish people. That evening she strode into the vestry and invited him and Helen to stay at Park Place the following night. Ridley accepted the invitation, one of many which were to come his way from the great and the good of his newly adopted country.

Why this substantial lady happened to be in a non-conformist chapel in Henley-on-Thames that evening when she had her very own chaplain to conduct services for her on Sundays at Park Place we may never be quite sure. She certainly was a non-conformist Christian with a heart for Israel and a Jewish Christian speaker would have been a great attraction, but why the clandestine visit? Sadly, most of the Herschell family correspondence was lost many years ago in a fire in London. What remains are mostly quotations from their eldest daughter Ghetal in memorials of her mother and father written many years after the events. Often, like this one, they were events that happened even before she was born.

The impression seems to be given by Helen that things happened purely by providence, and there is no doubt that God's hand was in the events that followed. But modern computer records reveal that Helen herself was distantly related to the Fuller-Maitlands through the marriage in 1829 of her cousin Ann Maria to Joseph Maitland. And Joseph, a member of the Scottish side of the vast Maitland family, happened to be the third cousin of Ebenezer Fuller-Maitland. Not for the first time God may have been offered a helping hand by a member of the ruling class of the British Empire.

Ridley had won over Mrs Fuller-Maitland but at that time he had made no serious study of theology, although he was very familiar with both the Old and the New Testaments. He would just speak from the heart, after prayerful study, and the results were often astounding. Whether he was in the pulpit or simply talking about his faith to people face to face Ridley spoke with a power far beyond his own academic ability. At Park Place he was requested to read and explain a chapter of the Bible at family worship. It seems everybody there felt that "he brought something new to them - something which all the religious instruction they had hitherto received had not given them, views of the love of God, which were like a revelation to them." The minister, Mr Bolton, speaking of a previous encounter at Worlingham Hall in Suffolk, said, "The impression made upon me by the whole strain of his conversation was, that I had never heard anyone's tone and talk so like the Epistles of John - it was all love. What he said I cannot recollect, but the impression abides still."

Worlingham Hall was owned by the family of Olivia Sparrow, another wealthy Christian lady, of whom we shall hear more. And the long friendship with Mrs Fuller-Maitland would lead to a very interesting conclusion many years later.

But for now the honeymoon was nearly over, and it was time to leave the good life and get back to work. Being the cousin of the wife of a third cousin of Ebenezer Maitland may have got Ridley an audition, but it didn't entitle them to a free ride. They would return to London and the house at Kensington, but only for a few more weeks. Their family accommodation there was required by the returning occupiers, Mr & Mrs Simon[65], and the Herschells would have to look for another home in Ireland. They would be leaving behind six Jewish enquirers and four newly baptised Jewish residents. Others had moved on already, to Birmingham, Manchester and even Dublin to find work and perhaps a better life. Ridley and Helen would seek them out to give them encouragement in their new faith, and help them wherever they could. Now the work would really begin, and at Christmas 1831 they left for Dublin.

---

[65] Erasmus H. Simon and Barbara A. Simon

Chapter 13

The snow lay hard and crisp upon the ground; and spread over the thickly-strewn mounds of earth, so white and smooth a cover that it seemed as if corpses lay there, hidden only by their winding sheets. Not the faintest rustle broke the profound tranquillity of the solemn scene. Sound itself appeared to be frozen up, all was so cold and still.

Charles Dickens, *The Pickwick Papers*

Happily for the Herschell's the white Christmas of 1830 which had inspired this scene from The Pickwick Papers would not be repeated in 1831. But travelling north would still not be easy, or comfortable. Winters in England were still very cold and travel was generally by unheated stagecoach. Only a rug over the knees and a muffler would protect them and it could still take twenty-four hours to travel from London to Liverpool and another twelve to cross the notoriously rough Irish Sea to Dublin. And although it was seven years since George Stevenson's railway engine *Locomotion* had travelled from Darlington to Stockton with 450 passengers at fifteen miles per hour, it would be several more years before his line from London to Birmingham would be in service.

Meanwhile over thirty horse drawn stagecoaches a day were covering the route from the capital to the Midlands at an average speed of ten miles an hour and for each coach four fresh horses would be needed about every ten miles. This achievement was mostly due to John McAdam's tarmac roads, a vast improvement on the rutted tracks of the previous century, and the revenues raised by the unpopular turnpike tolls. As the roads improved famous stagecoaches like the *Independent Tally Ho* could make the 119 mile journey from London to Birmingham in under twelve hours, an average speed to rival Stevenson's new-fangled steam engine, but not for long. The hundred year supreme reign of the railway was about to begin.

Ridley and Helen themselves were to have a taste of things to come in this new railway age when they got to Manchester, but their first stop by coach was the Midlands and the great city of Birmingham, soon to be the manufacturing heartland of the world. A letter written at that time by Helen sums up the sad state of many Jewish people in that part of England at the time: "Our first day's journey was to Birmingham; there I may say my dear husband's missionary labours among his brethren first commenced. After making it for some time a subject of prayer, he at length saw his way clear to go among them . . . He knew there were many Jews resident in Birmingham, besides those wanderers who resort thither to get their jewellery boxes replenished; but he was ignorant of the name or abode of any one of them. He set out one evening with no other clue than the recollection of the name of a little public house, to which he remembered some of the members of the Institution who had been in Birmingham, said the Jews resorted. He walked towards it, and while doing so saw one standing at the door of a small shop. He gave him the usual salutation in Hebrew of "Peace be unto you" was immediately recognised as a brother, and asked to walk into the parlour. Here he spent some time in conversation with the Jew and his wife, chiefly on the present low and degraded state of their nation as to spiritual things. Being English Jews, he found them as usual very ignorant, and little acquainted with their own Scriptures. From them, however, be learnt the names and addresses of several Jewish families, and among others heard of one family whom he had known in his unconverted state, and when they were in more prosperous circumstances. He went to call upon them; the husband was absent, but he was very kindly received by the wife, although she knew of his baptism. Not to make my story longer than necessary, I shall merely add that he went to the synagogue on Friday evening, accompanied one of the Jews home to his lodgings, and there spoke for a considerable time to six Jews on the work of Messiah, declaring his belief that Jesus of Nazareth was He. Another evening he expounded the Scriptures to nine Jews and Jewesses, who were all very attentive. At the request of the Jewess above mentioned he took me to call on her one day. She received me very kindly. She appeared pleased when I told her that I considered myself a Jewess; indeed to be treated by a Christian without contempt seemed very gratifying to her feelings."

Of course, it was never going to be easy for anybody, Jew or Gentile, to be a committed Christian. From the day they stoned the Jewish martyr Stephen[66] things didn't look good for those who accepted this Jesus as their Lord and Messiah. But for a Jew who made that decision there were, and still are, additional perils. Not only were they likely to be cut off from their own community and even their own family, as Ridley had been, they were often not even welcomed into the Gentile society which supposedly identified itself with Christianity. Not a very good response to the injunction in Leviticus 19:33, "When an alien lives with you in your land, do not ill-treat him."

The Jewish people were called by God to be a "holy nation"[67] set apart from the world to serve God and be an example to the world:

"Nations will come to your light, and kings to the brightness of your dawn."[68]

This holiness or separation might range from total isolation from the rest of the world to the simple observation of festivals that were not recognised or understood by the local people. An irrational fear often gripped the nations among whom the Jews lived for nearly two thousand years. They were different, and that was a threat.

But Christians too were called to take on the same mantle of holiness as part of their Jewish inheritance in Jesus. They were to be a royal priesthood, a holy nation belonging to God, "that you may declare the praises of him who called you out of darkness into his wonderful light."[69]

But there were times when more darkness than light came out of the Church to greet these strangers in their land, even though the Church's roots were planted firmly in Judaism.

The Jews no longer had a home of their own after their expulsion by the Romans from Israel in AD 70. In most places, apart from perhaps France and

---

[66] Acts 7:56

[67] Exodus 19:6

[68] Isaiah 60:3

[69] 1 Peter 2:9

the United States, they didn't even have full citizenship rights and restrictions on Jewish immigration to England would only have been lifted in 1826, shortly before the young Haim officially arrived in August.

Bars to Jewish progress were gradually being lifted in England, though the *Jewish Emancipation Act* allowing Jews finally to enter Parliament would not be passed until 1858. Interestingly one of Ridley and Helen's children would be enabled one day to become a British Member of Parliament and eventually Lord Chancellor of England as a result of these reforms. But that was many years ahead.

Having ministered to as many Jewish converts as they could find in Birmingham and even spoken about his Christian faith in a synagogue, Ridley and his wife needed to move on to Manchester for the last stage of their land journey before sailing to Ireland.

Helen would write with restrained excitement: "We went from Birmingham to Manchester, where we only remained one night, and proceeded the next day by the far famed railway to Liverpool."

The impressive Manchester to Liverpool railway line had opened in September 1830. As Ridley and Helen walked towards the new and imposing Liverpool Road Station, the first railway station in the world, they could hardly have imagined where this revolution would lead. Two of their granddaughters, Agnes and Muriel, would see a tragic World War fought in line with railway timetables. But only Muriel would live to see millions of Jews transported to their destruction in railway trucks and carriages by the Nazis. Among them would almost certainly be the remaining Jewish population of Strzelno, her grandfather's home town.[70]

---

[70] "On the eve of WWII, there were a small number of Jews in Strzelno. Their fate is not known. However, we know that the Jews of Mogilno (the town and the county) were among the first to be deported by the Germans to the *Generalgouvernement* territory." *Hebrew Pinkas Hakehillot,* Yad Vashem, Jerusalem, Israel

The Yad Vashem Archives has microfilmed documents in German from the office of the *Chef der Sicherheitspolizei und des Sicherheitsdienstes Umwandererzentralstelle Posen* (UWZ) with correspondence and surveys concerning the district of Mogilno and planned deportations, 1939-1940. One of the frames in the microfilm is a survey of district Mogilno giving an ethnic composition of the population. mentioning one Jew in Strzelno/Strelno. (*Courtesy of Yad Vashem, Jerusalem, Israel*).

When the Herschells finally arrived in Liverpool they were, as their daughter Ghetal later rather understated it, "in some difficulty how to continue their journey to Dublin" They were, not to put too fine a point on it, broke.

But like his contemporary and fellow worker among the Jewish people, George Müller, Ridley Haim Herschell learned to depend on prayer to fund the work which God called him to do. Müller built and ran his now famous orphanage at Ashley Down near Bristol without knowing from one hour to the next where the money was to come from, but it always came. And so it was no surprise to the Herschells when a complete stranger in Liverpool gave them a cheque for twenty pounds, begging them, according to their daughter Ghetal, "to accept it as an offering to the Lord's work in which they were engaged." They would sail for Dublin after all.

Chapter 14

Deasy halted, breathing hard and swallowing his breath.
I just wanted to say, he said. Ireland, they say, has the honour of being the only country which never persecuted the jews. Do you know that? No. And do you know why?

He frowned sternly on the bright air.
Why, sir? Stephen asked, beginning to smile.
Because she never let them in, Mr Deasy said solemnly.

James Joyce, *Ulysses*

Ireland can claim, with some justification, to be the only European country never to have persecuted the Jews, even though James Joyce, creator of Ireland's most famous Jew, Leopold Bloom in *Ulysses*, suggests, tongue in cheek, that it may have been because they never let them in in the first place.

A more likely reason was the small numbers of Jews who actually settled in Ireland. Perhaps the temptations and promises of America, tantalisingly just over the western horizon, were irresistible to them. Whatever the reasons, by 1818 it is said there were only two Jewish families left in Dublin. The rest had either emigrated or assimilated. There were just never quite enough of them to take root and become a perceived threat.

By the time Ridley and Helen arrived in the new year of 1832 there may well have been more Christian Jewish converts in Dublin than Orthodox Jews. In the three or four months they stayed there Ridley managed to make contact not only with some converts who had moved from London but also with the tiny Jewish community. He was also able to help and encourage local Gentile Christians to learn more about the Jewish roots of their faith. But there were, apparently, disappointments. "My parents left Dublin after a stay of three or four months", writes daughter Ghetal, "having partly succeeded in the object which induced them to go there." The fact that their success was only partial may have been due to lack of support from Erasmus Simon back in England. Things were not going well in Kensington and some inmates resented being made to fend for themselves while the new institute in Bethnal Green was supporting its inmates over an entire three year programme.

Another factor was Helen's unexpected and serious illness during their stay in Ireland. Almost any illness was potentially life-threatening at that time. The western world was on the edge of some great discoveries in medicine, but Louis Pasteur was only ten years old, and Joseph Lister, who would discover antiseptics, was still only a child. There was much yet to be achieved in this age of progress. The Dublin School of Anatomy, Medicine and Surgery would open that very year but it would be another ten years before the introduction of anaesthetics and another ten until, in 1853, Doctor John Snow would bravely administer chloroform to Queen Victoria in her confinement.

But something beyond medicine and almost beyond her doctor's understanding got Helen through to continue the work she had been called to do. She had, writes Ghetal, "manifested such childlike faith, and so much real love to the Saviour, that the physician who had attended her refused any remuneration, saying it was a privilege and honour to wait upon such a devoted servant of God." Probably the most pressing reason for returning to England in the spring of 1832 however was that Ridley and Helen were expecting their first child. They would need to find settled work and a home for the baby that would be born towards the end of the year. And so they arrived in Woolwich, once a fishing village but now a busy town on the edge of London, divided between Kent and Essex by the River Thames. Erasmus Simon was on his own.

Chapter 15

"Mrs. Joe," said I, as a last resort, "I should like to know -

if you wouldn't much mind - where the firing comes from?"

"Lord bless the boy!" exclaimed my sister, as if she didn't quite mean that, but rather the contrary. "From the Hulks!"

"Oh-h!" said I, looking at Joe. "Hulks!"

Joe gave a reproachful cough, as much as to say, "Well, I told you so."

"And please what's Hulks?" said I.

Charles Dickens, *Great Expectations*

The lifetime of Ridley Haim Herschell coincides almost exactly with what is often called The Age of Reform in England. The period from about 1820 to 1860 (when Dickens wrote *Great Expectations*) was at once a time of life-enhancing progress and almost primitive social horror. While Helen could take Mr Shillibeer's new horse-drawn Omnibus to town from Woolwich or even consider buying a new-fangled sewing machine from France, down the road on the Thames, along whose banks they had strolled at Henley, lurked the dark, notorious prison ships, the Hulks. Crippled warships without sails or rigging, their masts removed, lying shameful and silent. They had been converted to hold thousands of prisoners awaiting transportation to Bermuda, Botany Bay or Van Dieman's Land[71].

As long-term prisoners they could wait years to be shipped out of the country, and while they waited they would labour at the Woolwich Arsenal, the state arms factory. For this they were paid a penny a week to spare them the ultimate indignity of actually being slaves. Although slavery officially ended in Britain in 1807 it would not be abolished in the colonies until 1834, and for a couple more years the wretches in the Hulks could consider themselves better off than their African brothers and sisters in the West Indies. The prisoners

---

[71] Tasmania

were not actually owned for life, as personal property, as the slaves were. In fact the prisoners had some hope, however slim, of even making their fortune in the New World when they were finally released there.

The cannon fire heard from across the marshes by Pip, the hero and narrator of *Great Expectations*, meant that one of these prisoners had escaped. This would have been unusual in the 1830s because the prisoners were chained by the legs and guarded day and night. The punishment, if they were recaptured, would be most severe. On board the *Justina,* moored at Woolwich when the Herschells arrived, the infamous Cat o' Nine Tails, a whip of nine twenty-four inch knotted cords, was still the punishment of choice. Prisoners could die of the wounds inflicted by the Cat.

The Hulks continued to be used until 1859, and Transportation to the colonies wasn't formally abolished until 1868. But the Thames was also home to happier craft. Steam ships, barges and boats of all kinds plied their trade on that busy, exciting river known as Old Father Thames. Even into the mid 1960s to travel on the Woolwich Free Ferry was the nearest thing to a sea voyage for many Londoners. The coke driven paddle steamers chugged across the Thames between Woolwich on the Kent side and North Woolwich in Essex, passing and re-passing each other like great ironclad dancers. All day and into the evening they crossed in a short, sweeping *pas de deux,* churning up the murky grey-green waters of the busy river.

Just down the road from the ferry terminal on the south side, close to the Arsenal, is New Road, now Woolwich New Road, and number twenty-three is the address of The Woolwich Development Agency. But in 1832 it was about to become the new home of Ridley and Helen Herschell with their newborn baby daughter, Ghetal. Ridley had named her after his mother as he had promised. An old friend, a guest at the wedding in Kensington, would write to Ghetal many years later, "When you were first placed in your mother's arms, you were welcomed with these words – 'You are not mine, you are the Lord's, and I am only His steward.'[72]

---

[72] *Far above Rubies, Memoirs of H. S. H., by her Daughter.* Edited by R. H. Herschell, 1854

But Woolwich was not just to be home for the new family. According to Ridley it would also become "a home for wayfaring Jews"[73]. These were Jewish travellers who supported themselves by selling small wares and trinkets and Ridley believed that if they had a home where they could go and take a meal, or sleep for a night, they might have an opportunity of seeing the "practical working of Christianity."[74] Helen would later write of these hard times: "If you wish to see me, in your mind's eye, in the scene of my future duties, you may picture me sitting in what I have now learned to reckon a large room; that is, one about twenty-two feet by sixteen. Here you may imagine me sitting with no carpet, and a large deal table in the middle of the room, the sides adorned with chairs of every possible colour and pattern. Here we shall take all our meals, and here, in a winter evening, if we live to see it, we shall sit with our adopted children."[75]

The adopted children were to be the Jewish wayfarers.

Helen was pregnant again and still in poor health. The possibility of not living through one of the harsh winters of the 1830s was very real. But she would continue to draw on the faith that brought her through in Ireland and, writing to a friend about the hardships of her new life, she says: "I trust God has long since made me willing to be useful in any way He chooses; either as a hewer of wood, or drawer of water."[76]

Before Ridley himself could start serious work in Woolwich there was some unfinished business back in Poland. He had received a letter from his father proposing a meeting in north Germany. Ridley desperately wanted to see Judah again, perhaps for the last time, but he did not want him to travel the four hundred miles from Strzelno to Hamburg. So he wrote to a friend and benefactor asking for help to enable him to meet his father back in Poland:

---

[73] *Ibid*

[74] *Ibid*

[75] *Ibid*

[76] *Ibid*

23 New Road

Woolwich,

June 11 1832

My dear friend,

I know that you as a father of a worthy family will be able to sympathise in my joy, I therefore think it right to inform you of what the Lord has done for me. Namely, I received last week a letter from my beloved father, who declared to me that my last letter had melted his heart, and that he can no longer withhold his fatherly affections from me...[77]

The "dear friend" Herschell wrote to in Liverpool in the early summer of 1832 was James Cropper, Quaker, philanthropist, anti-slavery campaigner and director of the new Liverpool and Manchester Railway. Cropper may have become his patron through their mutual connection with the abolitionist sympathiser Hannah More. Whatever their relationship it seems that Cropper would be funding the trip to Poland. He may also have provided the tickets for the Herschell's train ride on his railway and probably sent the mysterious "gentleman" Helen refers to who gave them the twenty pound cheque to get to Ireland. But these details are now lost. What is also lost in this letter is any acknowledgement of Helen's major contribution to the reconciliation with his father. All Ridley could manage to say about his highly intelligent, multi-lingual, three months pregnant wife was, "I leave my dear Helen here at Woolwich." Which was probably quite affectionate for the times.

In fact, Helen had by now become fluent in Hebrew and had written to Ridley's father in that language explaining his son's new Messianic Christian faith. This followed a visit to London by one of Ridley's cousins who reported home that Haim had not yet quite become an "idolater", the word applied by Polish Jews to the life and worship of Roman Catholics in Poland at that time. Daughter Ghetal describes the response to Helen's plea in these dramatic lines:

---

[77] Adam Matthew Publications Ltd, Marlborough, Wiltshire

"The arrival of this letter in the Polish home caused great astonishment. 'Is she, or is she not a Jewess,' they asked themselves; the Hebrew letter, the love for the Jewish nation, the whole tone of the communication was so utterly different from any of the phases of Christianity with which they were familiar, that they could scarcely believe the writer to belong to the oppressing race, and they almost began to indulge the hope that rumour had spoken falsely, and that their Haim had not been baptised."

But why did Helen seem to be so different to other Gentiles they knew? Why did the family hope she may even have been a Jewish girl? And why would they be so relieved if Haim had not really experienced the perceived horror of a Christian baptism? To begin to find the answers we need to go back to that little girl torn from her family home and forced to be baptised. This incident was not an isolated Herschell family tragedy that needed to be dealt with and perhaps respectfully closed. And these were not a band of insane renegade nuns who would today find themselves imprisoned and branded as monsters by the press. The treatment of this Jewish child was a way of life for the Jews of Poland, Russia and much of 19th century Europe. "In England", wrote Herschell in 1834, "although the Jews labour under certain civil disabilities, yet justice is as open to them as to the Gentiles. In Poland and Russia it is far otherwise; they are oppressed on every side, yet dare not complain; they are robbed and defrauded, yet obtain no redress."[78]

The hatred often shown to the Jewish people, dispersed around the world since the destruction of the Jerusalem Temple in AD 70, has been thoroughly documented elsewhere, and this is not the place to look at it again in any detail. A few examples from Herschell himself must suffice to give an impression of the daily terror Jews lived under in his time as well as many centuries before and for over a century to come.

In 1834 Herschell wrote: "The children in the streets often throw stones at the most respectable Jews, and call them opprobrious names. If a Christian, I

---

[78] *A Brief Sketch of the Present State and Future Expectations of the Jews*, Ridley Haim Herschell, 1834

use this term not in its true meaning, but in the only sense in which a Jew can understand it; one who professes to be a follower of Christ; if a Christian, I say, comes into a coffee-house where he sees some Jews sitting, his pious zeal prompts him immediately to utter some expression of insolent contempt, with which the proverbs and common sayings of his country amply supply him; such as, "I would rather kill a Jew than do so and so;" and many similar expressions of malevolence.[79]

During the time of Easter especially, which the Jews are aware is a festival in honour of Jesus, the malevolence displayed towards them exceeds all bounds. It is then hardly safe for them to walk the streets; and they are obliged to close their shops, and shut up the windows of their dwelling-houses, to prevent them from being broken.[80]

Several years ago, the emperor of Russia gave out a decree, that no Jew should remain at St. Petersburg, unless he were baptised; all the pious and conscientious Jews, therefore, were obliged to leave their possessions, and go to some other place; while those who were less so, paid a sum of money to a priest, to give them a certificate of baptism. It is customary to punish with the utmost rigour those Jews, who, being called Christians, continue to associate with their brethren, or to observe any of their own customs. They are either imprisoned for life, or sent to Siberia."[81]

Exactly a hundred years after Herschell wrote these words Leni Riefenstahl's film of the 1934 Nuremberg Nazi Rally, *Triumph des Willens* (Triumph of the Will) would present the German people to the world as the *Herrenrasse* (Master Race) and prepare the way for the destruction of six million of the Jewish *Untermenchen* (Low People) in the Holocaust. By 1940 the propaganda film *Der ewige Jude* (The Eternal Jew) would be showing the Jews as no more than migrating rats taking over a helpless Arian world.

The image of Christianity and so-called Christians which was presented to

[79] *Ibid*

[80] *Ibid*

[81] *Ibid*

the Jews of Strzelno then, and much later, bore little resemblance to the simple faith that was sent out from Jerusalem to the world on the Jewish feast of Pentecost. And it wasn't by any means restricted to the Roman Catholic majority either. Herschell writes: The bigotry of the Roman Catholics, who formed the bulk of the population, and the immoralities which prevailed as much among Protestants as among those who adhered to the old faith, were alike calculated to inspire them with hatred of a religion which produced such evil fruits." And one of Ridley's brothers, having looked into the forbidden New Testament, would confide: "Your answer to my last letter gave me much pleasure; especially your declaration, that those in our country who call themselves Christians, are not so; but are really heathens. After you told me what a Christian ought to be, and described to me what some of those you have the happiness of knowing in England, whom you denominate real Christians, truly are, I began to feel a desire to read the New Testament; and after a little hesitation, ventured to commence it. I cannot find expressions strong enough to convey to you how much I was astonished and overpowered at finding in it such holy and true doctrines; and such holy precepts inculcated on Christians, to make them wise unto salvation. But, dear brother, if there be only one New Testament, and if that be the one you gave me, how comes it, that the poor deluded creatures in our country think themselves the followers of Christ? And why do the Christians in England confine their zeal to the Jews? Why do they not send out missionaries to convert these poor heathens, who flatter themselves they are Christians, and to show them that they cannot be followers of Christ, when they live in the habitual commission of all that He forbids, and in the neglect of all that He commands? This might be serviceable to them, and would also serve to show the Jews, that the vice and impiety they see daily exhibited, is not Christianity."

So Ridley prepared for the long journey east. By sea to Hamburg, then by coach to Berlin and slowly onward to Strzelno. As he travelled he would visit synagogues in the major towns like Poznań and take advantage of their traditional hospitality to declare his belief that, "Jesus of Nazareth is the Messiah who has already fulfilled part of the predictions concerning Him, and is coming again to fulfil the remainder."[82] And though the declaration usually excited "much astonishment" Ridley declares, perhaps with some relief, "it was received with less opposition than I expected."

He must have often been conscious at these times of the words of Luke 4:16:

"He went to Nazareth, where he had been brought up, and on the Sabbath day he went into the synagogue, as was his custom. And he stood up to read."

Jesus was a Jew and on the Sabbath would himself go to *schul* (synagogue). So when the Christian Jew Ridley Haim Herschell finally arrived in his old home town of Strzelno he visited the synagogue. Like his master Jesus before him, and like any respectable Jewish visitor might be, he was called upon to read the chapter in the Law. Although Haim was *meshumid* (apostate) his family was still much respected in the town, and he was still an honoured guest, and a Jew. Ridley rose, opened the scroll and read:

"They travelled from Mount Hor along the route to the Red Sea, to go round Edom. But the people grew impatient on the way; they spoke against God and against Moses, and said, "Why have you brought us up out of Egypt to die in the desert? There is no bread! There is no water! And we detest this miserable food!"

Then the Lord sent venomous snakes among them; they bit the people and many Israelites died. The people came to Moses and said, "We sinned when we spoke against the Lord and against you. Pray that the Lord will take the snakes away from us." So Moses prayed for the people.

The Lord said to Moses, "Make a snake and put it up on a pole; anyone who is bitten can look at it and live." So Moses made a bronze snake and put it up on a pole. Then when anyone was bitten by a snake and looked at the bronze snake, he lived."[83]

---

[82] *Ibid*

[83] Numbers 21:5-9

As Haim rolled up the scroll his mind went back to Paris and his first fearful encounter with the New Testament. And the words of Yochanan, or John as he is known to the Gentile world, came back to him:

"And as Moses lifted up the serpent in the wilderness, even so must the Son of man be lifted up: That whosoever believeth in him should not perish, but have eternal life."[84]

And he remembered too his beloved mother. Here, close to her home where she had lived and died and raised her twelve children he made his peace with her. She who was, "jealous over us with a godly jealousy" would forgive him now. And before he left Poland for the last time Ridley Haim made a sort of peace with his father and grandfather. Helen writes: "My father-in-law sent me a very beautiful Jewish prayer book, and a plain gold ring that belonged to Ridley's mother. Upon the whole, he parted from them on comfortable terms; but to the last there were moments when the remembrance of his apostasy brought floods of tears."

[84] John 3:14-15 (KJV)

Chapter 16

How fast has brother followed brother
From sunshine to the sunless land!
William Wordsworth (1770–1850),
Extempore Effusion upon the Death of James Hogg

By the autumn of 1833, after only eighteen months the Herschells were on the move again. This time to Reading which lies directly west of London, in Berkshire at the junction of the Thames and its tributary the Kennet. Reading also happened to be home to the anonymous friend of Revd. Bolton, who they had met in Henley. Perhaps he had influenced the move because in Reading, according to Helen, they met with "a larger number of wayfarers than even at Woolwich" and the work was growing. They held a Shabbat service every Friday evening for both Jews and Gentiles, a big change from the exclusive days in Kensington, and both could hear the gospel preached in a Jewish context.

Ridley was preparing to publish his first book, *A Brief Sketch of The Present State and Future Expectations of The Jews*, Helen's health was improving, and baby Ghetal was fit and nearly two years old. Money was short and the work was demanding but things were going well for the little family. That is, until the truth came out about Joseph.

Joseph was one of Ridley's brothers. In fact Joseph was one of ten Herschell brothers. Six in all eventually came to England and lived for a time with Ridley and Helen. Most of them became naturalised British citizens and three of them, Louis, David Abraham and Victor would become Christian ministers like Ridley himself.

Helen received them all with unflinching love and kindness. Daughter Ghetal recalls: "My mother, instead of murmuring at additional burdens being thus placed upon her, rejoiced at the prospect of seeing any of her husband's family inquiring into the truths of Christianity; and she spared no pains or exertions to help them on, as regards the things of this present world, and that which is to come. Indeed, as one after another came to this country, she received each with warmest cordiality, and it was her joy and satisfaction to see them all embracing the Christian faith. Every one of them bears testimony to the kindness with which she welcomed them to her house, and acted throughout almost the part of a mother towards them. So desirous was she for their advancement in every way, that she would never indulge herself in speaking German with them, though she wished much to gain facility in conversing in that language; but she always insisted on making them speak English, as she said this was of far greater importance to them, than the other was to her."[85]

But brother Joseph's journey to Christian faith was to be longer and more painful, both for himself and for others.

It may have been the bright lights of London or just bad company, or perhaps what Helen called "too weak and pliable a disposition." Whatever the reason, Joseph had got himself into serious debt and with creditors hard on his heals he was planning, like so many before him, to leave them a long way behind and head for the New World of America. When Joseph left Reading Ridley was in despair. He was now under attack on all fronts, as a Christian, as a Jew, perhaps as an ungrateful immigrant who had been befriended by respectable members of British society. And the shame would extend to his equally respectable family back in Poland. Worse, at this time debtors could still be sent to jail, and the bleak Fleet Prison, made famous by Dickens in *The Pickwick Papers*, beckoned the unwary spendthrift. But, above all, Ridley dearly loved his brother. He tried many times and in many ways to bring the prodigal son of his father home, he even took up teaching Hebrew and German in an attempt to pay off his debts. But nothing worked, and soon Joseph set sail for America. He would never return.

Although Joseph wrote back to England for a while he gradually faded from their lives. But Ridley never forgot him and ten years later he happened

---

[85] *Far above Rubies, Memoirs of H. S. H., by her Daughter.* Edited by R. H. Herschell, 1854

to be in the United States speaking in Baltimore, Maryland. This was where Joseph had last been heard of, years before, so Ridley took time out from his many speaking engagements to make enquiries. After some time a message came from a Mr Reed, a clergyman who had known Joseph for a number of years. In fact he had been with him when he died, over two years before. Once again Ridley had lost the chance to say a final goodbye to a loved one. Now he hardly dared ask the question that was on his heart. Had Joseph mentioned him at any time? "Oh Yes", said the clergyman, "He constantly grieved and mourned over the trials he had caused you." And his faith? Had his faith in Messiah Jesus been renewed? These are the words of Ridley himself: "Mr Reed told me that he never witnessed a more decided and glorious change, or a deeper piety, than was exhibited by Joseph. Mr Reed said that he made private inquiry of those who saw him constantly, and the universal testimony was, that he spent whole days in reading the Bible and in prayer. He said it was quite a spiritual feast to visit Joseph, and that he had learned much from him. He watched by his bedside till he closed his eyes in death, a few minutes before which he looked at Mr Reed and said, 'Though I walk through the valley of the shadow of death, I will fear no evil.' Are not the ways of the Lord marvellous? What can I render unto Him for all His great benefits?"[86]

Early in 1834, shortly after Joseph had left for America, the Herschells moved from Reading to a "humble dwelling in Camden Town."[87] Charles Dickens' son describes Camden in 1879 as lying "to the north-east of Regent's Park on London clay, and is a moderately rented neighbourhood, with, as a rule, very moderate-sized houses. Quite small houses of six, eight, and ten rooms each can here be found, and it is, relatively to its distance from Charing-cross,[88] the cheapest neighbourhood, so far as rent is concerned, in London. [89]

In spite of their difficulties and the modest accommodation they arrived in

---

[86] *Ibid*

[87] Grove Street , now Arlington Road, Camden Town

[88] Charing Cross is generally thought of as the geographical centre of London, and is the point from which distances are measured.

[89] *Dickens's Dictionary of London*, Charles Dickens Jr., 1879

Camden "full of faith and hope" according to a friend. Helen and baby Ghetal had survived two winters and the family were still together. Ridley even opened a large infant's school "in a very poor, dirty, and low situation" where he expounded the Scriptures twice a week. "I had yesterday upwards of fifty persons," he said with some pride, "many workmen and workwomen, and also two or three ladies with fine trimmed bonnets!" But by the end of 1834 things had not gone so well, and friends in high places did not necessarily provide the answers. The old Institution up the road in Kensington had closed and Erasmus Simon had returned to the United States to work among the native Americans whom he believed to be descended from the lost tribes of Israel. Desperately short of funds Erasmus would make one more trip to England. Seriously ill with typhus fever, and against the advice of his physicians, he tried to sail back to America where his loyal wife Barbara awaited his return. But the voyage was too much for him. He died a few days out from Portsmouth and was buried at sea in the spring of 1835.

Edward Irving had died on 7th December and though the Herschell's had distanced themselves from the movement Helen stayed in touch until his untimely death.

And so, as Christmas dawned upon the Herschells, still struggling with Joseph's debts and with a new baby, Esther, to feed and clothe they shared the saddest Christmas they ever spent according to Ridley. Helen was beginning to write to friends about the possibility of leaving the country. They could, she believed, live cheaply among the large Jewish community in Altona, Germany, now part of Hamburg on the estuary of the river Elbe. So early in 1835 they left Camden Town and made plans to move on.

But first they would make a farewell tour of some of their upper class friends. Despite the 1832 *Reform Act* which attempted to redraw the social and political map of the United Kingdom, and despite the growth of an industrial *bourgeoisie* to compete with the landed gentry for power, the upper class patronage system remained alive and well in Herschell's day, at least in the arts and the churches. The wonderfully horrible world of Anthony Trollope and the chronicles of Barchester would exist for many years to come. It may even be that Herschell himself was the source for Trollope's sycophantic Jewish non-conformist minister, Joseph Emilius, in *The Eustace Diamonds*. This unflattering and cruel caricature of Herschell, if it is him, shows him later in life, seeking patronage, connections and even marriage and property among the upper classes. But Herschell had already turned down a secure living for himself and his wife and child as a minister in Scotland on the grounds that God was calling him to be an evangelist and not a pastor. In their present condition this was not the decision of an overly ambitious man. A friend of the family would write to Ghetal many years later: "A proposal was made to your father to enter into the ministry of the Established Church, with prospects of advancement that would have freed your parents from many cares, and placed them in a position where, as of customary and acknowledged right, associations such as I have alluded to might have been shared. I witnessed, on that occasion, the deep exercise of her soul; but it was lest your father should be prevailed on to forsake the ground he had conscientiously taken, for the sake of worldly advantages; and great was her joy when she found that no such concession of principle would be made. Once more, poverty and labour, change and uncertainty, were chosen for Christ's sake!"[90]

Helen herself wrote confidently to her friend in Scotland: "He does not feel by any means competent for the duties of the pastoral office. He has said from the first, that whatever God may be pleased to call him to hereafter, he is convinced that at present the office of an evangelist is the one to which he is called."

And God would honour that conviction in a rather surprising way.

[90] *Far above Rubies, Memoirs of H. S. H., by her Daughter*. Edited by R. H. Herschell, 1854

Chapter 17

'Of course, you know, the income will be very much reduced,' continued Mr Slope. 'The Bishop wished to be liberal, and he therefore told the government that he thought it ought to be put at not less than £450. I think on the whole the Bishop was right; for though the services required will not be of a very onerous nature, they will be more so than they were before. And it is, perhaps, well that the clergy immediately attached to the cathedral town should be made as comfortable as the extent of the ecclesiastical means at our disposal will allow. Those are the bishop's ideas, and I must say mine also.'

Anthony Trollope, *Barchester Towers*, 1857

It seems unlikely that even the manipulative Revd. Obadiah Slope in Trollope's masterpiece would advise the Creator of the universe about the time of the Second Coming of the Messiah, but in 1835 it might just have seemed possible. The twin dreams of certain leading Evangelical Christians at that time were the conversion of the Jewish people to Christianity and the establishment of a Jewish state in Palestine, which would be peopled by the said converts. The achievement of these objectives would, we must suppose, instantly fulfil prophecy and usher in the millennium and the rule of Christ on earth just a little earlier than planned. It has even been suggested that Zionism itself was "godfathered" by pre-millennial Christian zealots.

One such enthusiast was Lady Olivia Sparrow, daughter of the second Viscount and first Earl of Gosford, wife of the late Brigadier-General Robert Sparrow of Worlingham Hall, Suffolk, who had died of a fever at sea, and possessor, in her lifetime, of very large amounts of property. Married in 1797 and widowed just eight years later, Lady Sparrow was said to be a very eligible widow. One visitor from America, the Revd. Philander Chase, even wrote home to his wife in 1824 that "Lady Olivia is a grandmother, yet is apparently quite young and beautiful"[91] But the beautiful Olivia would never remarry, in all her eighty-eight years.

---

[91] *The Life of Philander Chase*, Laura Chase Smith, New York: E.P. Dutton and Co., 1903

It was early 1835 and the Herschells, Ridley, Helen, Ghetal and now Helen's "lovely Esther" arrived at Brampton Park[92], the vast Huntingdonshire home of Lady Olivia, where they were to stay for a few days. The sad decision to leave England had been made. They were all *en route* for Germany. "We both leave this country with much regret", wrote Helen, "but now feel it an imperative duty, from the difficulty of getting anything here to increase our means, and the impossibility of living upon them as they are."

It only remained to say farewell to their friends, at least for the time being. Ridley would teach or carry on the manual skills he had learned at the institute, and Helen, with three year old Ghetal and baby Esther, could keep house, like a good Jewish mother. Helen had nearly become the Jewish wife Ridley's family would have wanted. About that time she wrote to a friend in Scotland: "And now you will say, What are these poor wandering Herschells to do? Just what their fathers did before them. If they encamped in a place, and there was not much water, they struck their tents and pitched them elsewhere."

And so they talked and they dined and they discussed the state of the world with Olivia and the parish clergyman, "a truly pious and enlightened young man" according to Helen, and any other guests who might be passing through. Among their mutual friends had been the late Hannah More and the late Edward Irving.

They might well have discussed the prospects for Mr Brunel's Great Western Railway, Helen had been quite taken with their trip from Manchester to Liverpool, or even Mr Colt's new patent revolver. Olivia, who enjoyed theological discussion, might have sought Ridley's opinion on the new revival of Sabbatarianism in England and the observance of Saturday or Sunday as the Sabbath day of rest for Christians. Perhaps they rode a little, Lady Olivia had many horses and rode to hounds on her lands in Essex. Perhaps they danced, Ridley still loved to dance as he had in Berlin and Paris. Or maybe they played music in the evenings or read aloud to each other by the fire in the candlelight. The modest Helen would publish her own small book that year, but it is

---

[92] Now a Royal Air Force station

doubtful if she would have brought it to anybody's attention.[93]

During this time Olivia would almost certainly have been assessing Ridley's prospects. She had known the Herschells on and off for four years and was very fond of them, but his track record as an evangelist so far, on the face of it, was not too good. What could she offer him when in January he had turned down a comfortable living as a full-time clergyman? Did that not present opportunities for him to evangelise? Were there no needy Jews in Scotland he could reach out to?

Lady Olivia was sixty years old and, apparently, a wise, intelligent woman and a sound Christian. Ridley was still a young man of twenty-eight with a wife and two children to support. She didn't doubt his faith or his intellectual abilities but perhaps she may have thought a stay in Germany might bring him down to earth in a very harsh world that was merciless to those without the right connections. But Olivia decided to offer him one more opportunity to use his gifts in a practical situation in England. The Herschells may have put their trust in the Lord but Lady Olivia would give the Lord a hand, and the Lord appears to have taken it.

In December of 1834 Olivia had opened a school for poor children in Leigh, a small fishing village on the Thames estuary. She also happened to be Lady of the Manor there and, although her home, Leigh Manor, was rented out at the time to a tenant farmer, she had retained the right to hunt on the land.

Education was expensive and hard to come by in these times just before the dawn of the Victorian era. These were the days of the so-called ragged schools set up for poor children to receive some form of free or very cheap schooling. The system would be more formally established by the Christian philanthropist Lord Shaftesbury under the Ragged School Union in 1844 and this would be the model for the poor until the reforming *Education Act* of 1870.

Whether as a result of bad management or lack of support Lady Olivia's

---

[93] *The Child's Help to Self-examination and Prayer,* Helen S. Herschell, 1835

school and other charitable institutions in Leigh had already, according to Helen, "fallen into great disorder"[94] and needed urgent attention. Would Ridley and Helen perhaps like to take on the task for a trial period of two months?

There is little doubt a deal had been struck between Helen and Olivia behind the scenes. But Ridley was the boss, even though he was ten years younger than Helen. He would decide, and his decision would be final and absolute. He would not be swayed by these conspiring women.

"Thither, in 1835, my parents went", wrote Ghetal twenty years later of the family's relatively short journey to the village of Leigh.

---

[94] *Far above Rubies, Memoirs of H. S. H., by her Daughter.* Edited by R. H. Herschell, 1854

Chapter 18

And Jesus, walking by the sea of Galilee, saw two brethren, Simon called Peter, and Andrew his brother, casting a net into the sea: for they were fishers. And he saith unto them, Follow me, and I will make you fishers of men.

The Bible, Matthew 4:18-19

Leigh-on-Sea today is a very pleasant and bright town looking out to sea from the mouth of the blue-grey Thames, about thirty-five miles from London. A fast road and the railway now connect it to the capital for commuters. And the bright lights and busy town-centre shops of Southend-on-Sea, its mile and a quarter Pleasure Pier stretching out into the estuary, are a short bus ride away. All far removed from the Leigh of 1835.

The school had been built on Hall Road, now The Broadway, close to the Anglican Church and the comfortable house they had moved into. But far below the town, on the north bank of the River Thames, was the notorious fishing village.

"The village itself", wrote Helen, "was in a condition of the deepest demoralisation; so much so, that the neighbouring farmers would not permit their daughters to go into it."

A description of the people by Helen at the time not only shows a population on the verge of anarchy but highlights the vast gap between rich and poor, between the better off classes and these, the lowest in the pecking order of society. Ridley and Helen considered themselves poor when they thought of moving to Germany but that was only a relative poverty, real enough, but within their own class. They always had the choice to move on and recover their fortunes. The poverty, ignorance and moral degradation they met with in Leigh was unlike even that of the East End of London which Ridley had experienced but where, certainly among the poor Jews, strict moral standards were maintained and education was available to most. It would challenge the Herschells and change their lives and the lives of the fishermen forever.

Since the local clergyman, Edward Newton Walter, Rector of St. Clements church, had all but given up on the fishermen and was "very remiss in the discharge of his duties" Ridley took the opportunity to hold a service in the village on Sunday evenings, leaving much of the school work to Helen.

"He began last Sunday," Helen wrote, early in 1835, "and was much pleased to find a great many uncouth-looking personages, dressed in white flannel waistcoats, without coats at all. These were the fishermen in their home costume." "Many of these", adds daughter Ghetal with the rather condescending air of her time and class, "had never entered a place of worship in their lives."

These were certainly tough, hard-drinking and violent men. The constant threat of death at sea, especially in the long cold winters of the 19th century, and the grinding hard labour had created a breed of men who were fearless in the face of authority and godless in their daily lives. Philip Benton in his 1880's *History of Rochford Hundred* reports: "The Incumbent of St. Clement's Church warned him (Herschell) not to go down into the place, such was its untoward character."

And yet, here were many of them, standing on a Sunday evening, before this small young man from a land they had never heard of and of a race despised by many. And he held them all, brothers of those Galilean fishermen of old, with just the Bible in his hand and the message of salvation it contained in his heart. And they listened.

One of the toughest of these hard men was twenty-one year old Michael Tomlin. Michael was a big man and a heavy drinker who was feared and respected, even by his fellow fishermen. He had achieved a feat few could match. Long before the railway came to Leigh in 1854 the freshly caught fish would be transported to Billingsgate Market in London either by road or by barge up the Thames to Blackwall. But one day Michael had decided to deliver his catch personally and, along with a mate set out to row the thirty-five miles to the Capital. At some point on the arduous trip back his mate collapsed with exhaustion, totally overcome by the power of the river. But Michael would not give up. He took both oars and rowed alone, arriving in Leigh that same night, exhausted but unbeaten.

One Sunday evening this same Michael Tomlin turned up at Ridley's service with some of his friends, leaving his young wife Elizabeth at home. In a village with very little entertainment they had come along, they said, just to see what a Jew looked like.

Ridley began to speak, plainly, just as he always did to high and low, Jew and Gentile, of the love of God and the need for repentance. What happened next is vividly recounted in Stephen Frost Johnson's[95] book, *A Fisher of Men* published in 1945:

"And so it happened that as Mr. Herschell spoke in simple language, and told the story of the Cross, and the love of God in Jesus Christ, and what it had done for him, and would do for those young fishermen, Michael Tomlin came under deep conviction of sin, suddenly picked up his hat and went out and down to his cottage. Arriving there, he began to pace the room to and fro, in such a manner that his wife thought he had come from the public house and was under the influence of drink. Presently he fell down and his wife pushed him over, still thinking he was in the power of drink. But when she saw the tears streaming down his face she knew that something had happened. Michael looked up through his tears and said, "Betty, my life has been changed; the Jew has been telling me of the love of God and Jesus Christ and how He could alter my life.""

Helen had been right. God had called Ridley to be an evangelist. And he had called Michael Tomlin too, like Simon and Andrew before him, to be a "fisher of men". Like them Michael was to face many trials and the way would often be hard, but they would overcome through their faith. The illiterate fisherman, my great great grandfather, learned to read from the Bible and to preach the gospel to anybody who would listen. And many people would listen. But he never wrote down his sermons, he just spoke from the heart after careful study and prayer, like his friend Ridley Herschell. One day, long after the Herschells had left, he would be invited to build a church in the area

---

[95] Stephen Frost Johnson (1876-1959)

and become a Methodist Minister. Michael and his wife Elizabeth[96], who had also accepted Jesus as her Lord and Saviour, would share their work together for another forty-three years, and they would have eight children. Only death could separate them in this life. In 1878 Betty died. Her headstone reads:

Elizabeth, the beloved wife of Rev. Michael Tomlin,
who departed this life May 10th 1878 aged 65 years.
She sleeps in Jesus.

Michael would live and work on alone for another twenty-four years. A Methodist church bearing his name remains alive and flourishing to this day not far from the old village[97]. Added to their shared headstone in the Anglican graveyard are these simple words,

In life and death - Jesus only.

---

[96] Elizabeth Turnnidge (1812-1878)

[97] Whittingham Avenue Methodist Church (Michael Tomlin Memorial), Southend-on-Sea, Essex

Chapter 19

If you become a teacher, by your pupils you'll be taught.

Oscar Hammerstein II (1895-1960), *The King and I*

Helen Herschell set to work at Lady Sparrow's schools with the enthusiasm and zeal she had practised at home in Scotland with her nine younger brothers and sisters, but now with the benefit of her thirty-seven years, and two young children of her own. One infant's school and two adult schools were established. Helen was a natural and progressive teacher who had educated herself way above most ladies of her generation and looked beyond the learning by rote associated with the times. "Not satisfied with merely visiting and teaching in them", writes Ghetal, "she assembled the teachers frequently at her house, in order that she might fit them to impart knowledge more efficiently to the children under their care. She also took a class every evening in the female adult school."[98] Ridley, naturally, would teach the men.

Inspired by her renewed contact with so many children Helen finished and published the small book that had been gathering dust for so long, *The Child's Help to Self-examination and Prayer.* "My chief desire", she wrote from Leigh in the summer of 1835, "is to endeavour to engage the mind of children in prayer; and to substitute the habit of attempting to raise their thoughts to God in prayer, for the mere formal repetition of certain words."[99]

Things were changing fast, not only in the world but in the little fishing village. Inspired by the commitment and courage of the Herschells, and in many cases by their new found faith, the fishermen and their families were becoming model citizens. A short extract from one of Helen's many letters sums up the amazing change of heart:

---

[98] *Far above Rubies, Memoirs of H. S. H., by her Daughter.* Edited by R. H. Herschell, 1854

[99] *Ibid*

"Before we came to Leigh, we were told that the people were so rude and unpolished, that those living in the neighbourhood almost feared personal incivility when they came among them. Instead of this, when we walk through the village we receive kind and respectful recognitions from every one. . . The wife of a clergyman, who lives some miles from this, told me that when one of the Leigh fishermen was asked lately why he did not swear as he used to do formerly, replied, that he had been better taught since he attended Mr. Herschell's lectures…. All this is great cause for thankfulness. There is nothing worth living for, but to be of some use in our day and generation."[100]

But not quite everything had changed in the social life of the Leigh sailors. The Lady of the Manor was back. The highlight of the year was to be the children's examinations. The old ways, Helen innocently calls them "the good old times"[101], still lingered on in the countryside at that time and Lady Olivia was expected to examine the children personally. This went on for a whole week and culminated in a grand public outdoor examination. Two hundred children gathered together under a large tent made from fishing boat sails which was erected by the men who had especially finished their work an hour early. A red, white and blue Union Jack flew on a long pole above it and the children sat down to a treat of tea and buns on the bright green lawn. Little enough by today's standards but a memorable feast in these gloomy times.

"It was truly delightful," Helen wrote with some of her old youthful excitement, "to see Lady Olivia, in the midst of her tenants, who united the old-fashioned veneration for superior rank with the warm and homely expressions of kindness; all anxious to gratify 'my lady' in every possible way, yet no one officious or impertinent."[102]

Some of these children would grow up to be the new reforming Victorians but, of the present adult company, only Michael Tomlin, with his big bushy beard spreading beneath shining eyes that seemed to reflect the light of his

_____

[100] *Ibid*

[101] *Ibid*

[102] *Ibid*

Saviour back to the world, only Michael would see that era through to the brave new world of the twentieth century, outliving even his Queen by two years.

Chapter 20

From every latent foe,

From the assassins blow,

God save the Queen!

O'er her thine arm extend,

For Britain's sake defend,

Our mother, prince, and friend,

God save the Queen!

United Kingdom National Anthem, Verse 5

Things could not have gone better for Ridley and Helen. They had settled down in their cottage with the two children, Ghetal and Esther, and all thoughts of Germany and exile were long forgotten. They were popular in the village and Helen was much loved by the fishermen's wives, many of whom had suffered terribly as a result of excessive drinking by their husbands and the domestic violence that so often followed.

Ghetal, who was only two years old at the time, recalls: "The villagers entertained a great affection for my mother; and when they saw her walking out, would run a long distance to open a gate for her. They showed their kind feelings, too, in their own simple way, by sending presents of fish and vegetables."[103]

But Lady Olivia Sparrow had other plans for her protégées. Ridley had done well, but now a new Anglican curate had been appointed to the parish, a hard-working, conscientious man, who took an interest in the village and its people. More importantly the new man would take over responsibility for the schools. The Herschells' work in Leigh was done. After only eighteen months their ministry and their prayers had transformed the people and when they

---

[103] *Ibid*

finally left, seven hundred of the fishermen subscribed a penny each to present Ridley with a Bible and Prayer Book.

By the summer of 1836 they had left Leigh and moved the ninety miles back up to Brampton, where Lady Sparrow had new opportunities awaiting her evangelistic team. This time it was a high profile job on Olivia's doorstep. She had bought herself a very large red house in Brampton High Street now known as The Grange Hotel and planned to open a free girls' school and an infants' school for the village.

Great things were expected, and great things would be achieved by the Herschells, but Ridley's heart was still in London among what he often called his "brethren according to the flesh", the Jewish people. He hadn't come all this way just to be a village schoolteacher, however noble that calling may have been. Lady Olivia had been instrumental in keeping him in England and the work at Leigh was clearly part of God's plan for him. But where would she move them next in her vast rural empire?

Olivia Sparrow could from all accounts be a rather difficult and unpredictable lady and in time would fall out with several local worthies. One day she would even build her own independent church in the village[104] having crossed the equally stubborn Rector of Brampton and been refused her own personal Anglican Chaplain.

Whether there was a falling out with Ridley we are not told. But after their move from Brampton little more is heard of Lady Olivia and the Herschell's find themselves once more under the patronage of the Fuller-Maitland family. Many years later, in the South of France on a journey to Rome, Ridley would diplomatically avoid a meeting with Lady Sparrow's daughter Millicent, by then the Duchess of Manchester, but we may never know why.

Of his Jewish brethren in London Ridley had written in 1834: "The same number of Jews as are resident in London (where I may safely assert four-fifths of the Jews in Britain are congregated), would, in any town on the Continent, have many pious teachers among them; and would possess

---

[104] Affiliated to the nonconformist Countess of Huntingdon's Connection

advantages of education that are unknown here. The Hebrew language is very little cultivated by them; and hence arises a great ignorance of Scripture, and consequently of all spiritual things. I say not these things to cast a stigma on any one; but I entreat my dear brethren, in England, to examine whether these things be not so: and to lay it to heart."[105]

London was calling Ridley, but for now they would settle in Brampton and by the spring of 1837 Helen was pregnant with their fourth child, their third, Mary, having been born in 1836. On 2nd November 1837 she gave birth to their first son, Farrer. His unusual name was taken from the surname of Oliver Farrer and his sister who had been two of Ridley's sponsors at his baptism. It may be an indication of his closeness to that family that he named his first son after them rather than his father, Judah. Ghetal had been named after Ridley's mother, Esther perhaps after Esther Fuller-Maitland of Park Place and Mary probably after his elder sister Miriam. But Judah would have to wait a little longer.

Meanwhile, beyond the small world of Brampton village, the old king, William IV, had finally died of pneumonia on June 20th leaving no legitimate children behind. So his niece, Alexandrina Victoria, a young girl of eighteen, became Queen of Great Britain and Ireland and was crowned a year later on 28th June 1838 in Westminster Abbey. On her accession to the throne in 1837 Helen Herschell wrote this touching song for the children of the infant's school in Brampton. It is called *The Infant Scholar's Address to the Queen*:

> Victoria! Victoria!
> We hail thy gentle, rule!
> Victoria, the patroness
> Of every infant school!
> The kings of old their people led
> To battles fierce and wild;
> 'Tis nobler far, with fostering care,
> To train each little child.
> When spring's return with primroses

---

[105] *A Brief Sketch of the Present State and Future Expectations of the Jews*, Ridley Haim Herschell, 1834

And violets fills the green,
We'll weave the pretty flowers to make
A chaplet for our Queen.
When summer brings the lovely rose
Again to deck the bowers,
We'll think of thee, when we behold
That fairest queen of flowers.
In autumn, when the yellow crops
Beneath the sickle bend,
We'll pray that peace and plenty may
Victoria's reign attend.
And when the winter's wind and snow
Beat cold against the door,
We'll think of her whose laws protect
The fireside of the poor.
We little children scarce can tell
What others mean by care;
But we are told 'tis sorely felt
By those a crown who wear.
Then when thy heart with sorrow swells,
What e'er thy troubles be,
Cast all thy care on Him who wore
A thorny crown for thee.
May God our Sovereign Lady grant
Long o'er this land to rule;
And children's children bless her name
In this our infant school.
If here we ne'er should see thy face,
May we hereafter meet,
Where thou wilt meekly cast thy crown
At our Redeemer's feet.[106]

This young, energetic and committed queen along with her millions of subjects, a quarter of the world's population at one time, was to see events and developments that would change the world beyond recognition. Great human progress was to be made, but the seeds of two horrific world wars and the near destruction of the Jewish people were also being sown in this awesome

---

[106] *Far above Rubies, Memoirs of H. S. H., by her Daughter.* Edited by R. H. Herschell, 1854

scientific and industrial world.

It was at this time of Great Britain's 'benevolent' world rule, tinged with not a little of that Victorian hypocrisy so pilloried by Dickens, that Helen began her amusing and gently satirical contributions to the *Christian Ladies' Magazine*, writing as the "elderly single gentlewoman" Martha Markwell.

"I am often led to observe", writes Martha in her first contribution, "the truth of the old adage, that the bystander sees more of the game than those who play. Many a time I foresee consequences for which the busy actors are little prepared; and I think I can often perceive the true motivation of an actor, which the performers imagine to proceed from one very different. The blindness of passion, the obstinacy of prejudice, and the selfishness of the human heart in its various manifestations, are objects of frequent and painful contemplation to me; for which I am only compensated, when I am enabled to benefit others by the results of my experience."

Helen managed to write her witty, perceptive and, presumably, anonymous *Bystander* column as well as bringing up her growing family, keeping house and teaching her newly acquired "young ladies". Meanwhile Ridley, concerning himself with the weightier matters which were on his heart, was preparing for yet another, and this time more dramatic and sometimes tragic, move. He would seek ordination, but not in the established Churches of England or Scotland, nor with the income that went with those appointments.

In 1835 Helen had written from Leigh: "My beloved husband is daily fitting more and more for the work to which I fully believe God has called him. On his preaching days he feels that he is really charged with 'the burden of the Lord;' when he has delivered it, he seems quite lightened of a load. I cannot but consider it a very wonderful thing that a foreigner, without premeditation, (though not without diligent and prayerful study), should be able to speak for upwards of an hour with fluency and eloquence, and often, with the feeling that he could go on for two hours longer did he think it expedient, which it clearly is not."

And by the time they had settled in Brampton, Ghetal recalls: "While at Brampton, my father, after much prayerful deliberation, decided on beginning to preach the Gospel in London. In order that he might have perfect freedom in doing so, and to keep him from all anxiety on her account and the children's, with regard to temporal matters, my mother determined to undertake the education of young ladies."

Although Ridley had been sent to Leigh and Brampton to organise the schools he had found himself taking more and more responsibility for running the churches. At Leigh it was a result of the Rector's absence and his fear of the fishermen, in Brampton a result of the minister's frequent ill health.

"Contrary to my expectations", wrote Herschell as he struggled to see the way forward, "I was compelled to take a ministerial and pastoral charge for about thirteen months. After this I was for two years and a half at Brampton, where also I only expected to have a charge over temporal affairs . . . But the minister being in ill health, was obliged often to be from home, and there again I was compelled to have a pastoral charge . . . God then pointed out to me clearly what He would have me do. Then the question was, In what way is it to be done? I was exceedingly anxious that neither Jew nor Gentile should be able to say to me, 'You have done this from mercenary motives;' that I had some worldly motive for entering into the Church, or taking a dissenting congregation. My desire in beginning here is simply to stand as a witness for Christ, and to expound the Scriptures of truth; and thus to labour in the service of Him 'who loved me and gave Himself for me.'"[107]

And so the break with Lady Olivia Sparrow finally came. The spire-like triangular stone obelisk at the end of the village with its hand pointing prophetically to London finally called them. In September 1838, with their four children, Ghetal, Esther, Mary and Farrer, they took up residence "in a pretty village near the Thames", writes Ghetal, "where they remained a year, while my father journeyed weekly to London to perform the duties he had taken upon himself in connexion with his chapel."[108]

His chapel, in fact the Church of Scotland's chapel, was at Founder's Hall, Lothbury, near the Bank of England. Founder's Hall had first been built in

---

[107] *Ibid*

[108] *Ibid*

1531 by the City's Company of metal founders in Lothbury. It was destroyed in the Great Fire of London as it swept through the narrow street and had to be rebuilt, with its new chapel, in 1669. Today, as then, Lothbury runs alongside the Bank of England but, sadly, nothing remains of the Hall or Ridley's chapel today except a blue plaque in the courtyard which reads:

In this court stood Founder's Hall

1531 to 1845

Rebuilt after the Great Fire 1666

The pretty village was Remenham, Oxfordshire, where the River Thames curves gently into Henley Reach, soon to become home to the now famous Henley Regatta. It lies, even today, hiding quietly in the shadow of Park Place, former home of Ebenezer and Bethia Fuller-Maitland.

Ridley's new position may have resulted from Ebenezer's banking connections in the City, but there may also have been a reconciliation between Helen and Thomas Chalmers. Founder's Hall Chapel would have effectively been in the gift of Chalmers as the newly appointed Professor of Divinity at Edinburgh University. In a letter dated December 1824 Helen had described him as "Our excellent friend Dr. Chalmers". Had Helen sacrificially renewed that friendship?

The Herschell's had long ago left behind the Rowites and the Irvingites and far from being a rogue, Ridley now had a growing reputation as an evangelist and preacher under Lady Sparrow's patronage. Helen had paid a high price for her disobedience and perceived rudeness to Dr Chalmers who had opposed the marriage.[109] So the time may have come for Chalmers to make some recompense. Three years earlier Ridley had been mysteriously offered a position in the Church of Scotland which he turned down. "The particulars of this proposal," wrote Ghetal, "are unknown to me." But they

---

[109] On 28th March 1831 Helen had offered to be examined under oath by Dr Chalmers regarding the behaviour of her friends at the time of her engagement. Her anger is evident and it would not have been received favourably by the Reverend Doctor: "I write this note to you under no feelings but that of desire that you should learn the truth, and regret that you should not have ascertained it before you expressed your decision so decidedly."

must have been well known to Helen.

And the Scots Church connection becomes even clearer as Herschell joins the ailing Robert Murray McCheyne, a former student of Chalmers, in setting up the British Society for the Propagation of the Gospel among the Jews.

The Herschells were back where they started, and Lady Olivia disappears quietly from their lives.

Chapter 21

"Sir, whatever the world may say of me, I have lived, and I die, a member of the Church of England. I pray you to bury me in your churchyard."

Charles Wesley to the Rector of St Marylebone, the Revd John Harley

Helen Herschell's relationship with the Fuller-Maitlands remains something of a mystery. She had been told in a letter from Esther Fuller-Maitland, whom she calls her friend, that Esther's parents, Ebenezer and Bethia, were finding it difficult to obtain a suitable governess for her two youngest sisters, Caroline and Jane Octavia. Helen offered her services.

"I immediately offered to take a cottage near them for myself and children, and attend them as a daily governess for six months," she wrote. "This offer was accepted in the most flattering manner......Mr Herschell has taken Founder's Hall Chapel, in Lothbury, near the Bank, and hopes to begin service in it in the middle of next month."[110]

Ridley would travel the thirty six miles from Henley to London by coach via Maidenhead, Colebrook, Hounslow and Brentford each week.

Writing in the 1920's J.A. Fuller-Maitland, the *Times* music critic and nephew of Esther, describes Helen as "greatly loved by her pupils"[111] but his assessment of Ridley is rather less enthusiastic and he dismisses him merely as "the Rabbi",[112] which had been his nickname, affectionately or otherwise, at Park Place. Ridley doesn't seem to have been quite socially acceptable to J.A. Fuller-Maitland, although he never actually met him, but Helen, whom he describes as "one of the Norfolk Mowbrays"[113] would, with their connections to the Duke of Norfolk, have been more to his liking.

---

[110] *Ibid*

[111] *A Door-Keeper of Music*, J.A. Fuller-Mailtland, 1929

[112] *Ibid*

[113] *Ibid*

But Helen was, in fact, one of the Leith (Edinburgh) Mowbrays, recently upgraded by her ambitious father from the more common Moubray, and was more closely related to the Fuller-Maitlands themselves than the Earl Marshall of England.

But Ebenezer and the matriarchal Bethia, as committed Non-conformist Christians and founder members of the so-called Clapham Sect would have been far more sympathetic to Ridley and his ministry. The Clapham sect were a group of English Christian social reformers based in Clapham, then a village near London, at the home of Henry Thornton and the famous slave trade reformer William Wilberforce. The group, which was not really a sect at all, had been centred around their Chaplain John Venn[114], charismatic Rector of Holy Trinity Church, Clapham. Most of the members were Evangelical Anglicans and Members of Parliament, as was Ebenezer himself.

Other members included Zachary Macaulay, Thomas Babington, James Stephen, and the ubiquitous Hannah More. Known, sometimes pejoratively, as the Saints, they were active between about 1790 to 1830 working for the abolition of the slave trade, improvement of prison conditions, and other humane legislation. They published a journal called the *Christian Observer* and helped to found several missionary and tract societies, including the British and Foreign Bible Society and the Church Missionary Society.

In November 1838, as Ridley began his work at the chapel in Lothbury, he summed up his calling in these simple words to a friend: "I feel it to be no small undertaking, but He who has hitherto holpen will continue His loving-kindness, for my trust is in Him. I am not at all careful about temporal difficulties, but my great difficulty is to realise God in my own soul, and to feel such a strong yearning over others as to be able to entreat them in the love of Jesus. It is a glorious work to be engaged in, but at the same time a very awful one. My motto as a minister is, 'As of God, in the sight of God, so speak I in Christ.'"

Like the reformer John Wesley, who had himself visited Leigh-on-Sea six

---

[114] 1759-1813

times to preach between 1748 and 1756, Ridley retained a great affection for the Church of England. He had many friends in the established church and it had cradled him in those early days after his conversion. But many problems remained. The paradox of infant baptism and adult conversion was a constant barrier as were the questions surrounding the validity of the Anglican priesthood, the incongruity of the burial service and its apparent promise of unconditional resurrection, and, most difficult of all, the restrictions of the parish system and the vow of canonical obedience. Ridley shrank from such a commitment: "I should have liberty to preach the gospel only where it is preached already, while every ungodly incumbent might shut me out from that field of spiritual darkness where he reigns supreme." The work at Lothbury occupied him for six months, but if he was to really be a full-time pastor, it would be on his own terms and in his own chapel. That opportunity would soon arise.

Chapter 22

There's a Friend for little children
Above the bright blue sky,
A friend who never changes,
Whose love will never die.

Victorian hymn, A. Midlane (1825-1909)

Long before Charlie Chaplin or Marie Lloyd trod the boards at Collins' Music Hall and in the days when Sadler's Wells was itself was still a vaudeville theatre, Providence Chapel, Islington, just round the corner from Mr Sadler's now famous wells, opened its doors to worshipers of the Calvinist Methodist persuasion.

It was April 1824 and Thomas Elliott had, under pressure from the New River Company who had leased him the land, finally built his long awaited chapel. Then as now the small classical-style building with its four ionic columns sat rather uncomfortably in the middle of a terrace of attractive three and four storey houses on one side of Chadwell Street, close to the Angel, Islington and the ceaseless clatter of horse-drawn vehicles.[115] Islington had by now become an established stopping point for stagecoach passengers heading for central London. Many would stay there overnight rather than risk meeting the highwaymen who still preyed on those unwary souls who travelled in the dark. They might even enter the city on one of the increasingly popular twenty-seater horse buses, or Shillys as they were briefly known after George Shillibeer who introduced them to London, and complete their journey under cover, especially if they had been travelling "outside" in the open air.

Over the decades Providence Chapel would become known as Mount Zion Chapel and, much later, Angel Baptist Church. Today, in the twenty-first

---

[115] The chapel would feature in Dicken's *David Copperfield* as the place of David's marriage to Dora.

century, it looks rather neglected and a brief notice informs the world that Angel Baptist Church "closed for public worship on 27th October 2002."

But in April 1839 the chapel was far from neglected. After fourteen years of splits and schisms among its various Christian occupants, the Revd. Ridley Haim Herschell and his wife, now expecting their fifth child, entered into a six-year ministry together at what would be known as Chadwell Street Chapel.

On 7th September 1839 a second son, Ridley Judah was born at their new home, above a shop at number two Edward Terrace, Chalk Road, Islington.[116] In the summer of 1841, during the first Opium War in China, a powerful British naval force would sail northward and seize five seaports including Shanghai. Ridley Judah's future would be sealed on that day.

Edward Terrace, like so much property in London at that time, was new and reflected the growing prosperity of many of its genteel occupants. Nearly every building surrounding them had been built by developers during the previous ten years as the great metropolis spread out into the green fields of Middlesex and beyond.

Living close to the Regent's Canal and the site of the old smallpox hospital at Battle Bridge, where King's Cross Station would soon be built, the Herschells were back within reach of central London and the Jewish people. And the hard work continued to bear fruit. By late October 1839 Helen was able to write: "I will now give you a report of our chapel, as I know how much you are interested in it. It is usually well filled in the morning, and most unpleasantly crowded at night . . . Some interesting cases have occurred of persons who had been living in the entire neglect of public and private worship, who seem to have been awakened by my dear husband's ministry. This is a great call for thanksgiving."

Things were going well and they had many opportunities to reach out to the rapidly growing North London community. The cold winter of 1839-40 lingered on into March, though thankfully for the poor the Thames did not freeze over as it had in 1837-38 when temperatures in London had dropped to

---

[116] Now incorporated into the Caledonian Road

minus sixteen centigrade. Naturally the children had coughs and colds and Helen's sciatica grew worse by the day. But more worrying than all this was the rash and sore throat that five-year-old Esther had developed in the middle of that month. Although he had never practised medicine, apart from issuing simple remedies to the poor in Leigh and Buckden, Ridley's medical training in Berlin warned him of the worst possible diagnosis of these symptoms. He examined Esther. He opened her small mouth and looked at her tongue.

"Scharlach", he whispered, his English deserting him as the familiar German word came to his lips, *"Scharlach!"*

"Scarlet fever?" said Helen, knowing the awful certainty of the contagious disease. There was little hope. The doctor was called and confirmed the diagnosis. Three days later, on Friday 20th March 1840, the lovely Esther died.

"I am thankful to say," Helen wrote shortly after the death of her beloved daughter, "that my mind is entirely resigned to the removal of my lovely Esther; and though the sudden disappearance of such a sweet and interesting child from our family circle was a bitter pang, yet, if a wish of mine could recall her, I would not venture to do so. When I remember the many painful struggles that are to be gone through before the heart is really given to God, I can look with complacency on her as being already safe in her eternal home. I should have felt very differently had she been fifteen or twenty years older, and been as suddenly cut off, while yet halting between two opinions, knowing she ought to live for another world, and desiring to live for this world."[117]

Death was an ever-present reality for these early Victorians. The response of Christians to sickness and mortality was always, and should perhaps still be, tied inextricably to the doctrine of regeneration, of being born again:

"For you have been born again, not of perishable seed, but of imperishable, through the living and enduring word of God."[118]

We can only imagine Ridley's own agony from these words he wrote

---

[117] *Far above Rubies, Memoirs of H. S. H., by her Daughter.* Edited by R. H. Herschell, 1854

[118] 1 Peter 1:23

during a previous illness of one of his children in December 1838. He remains silent about the death of Esther: "The illness of my beloved infant was sent to me just when I needed it. I received it as a blessed message from my heavenly Father. Bitter as the trial is to hear the moans of a beloved babe, yet sweet is the consoling thought that, as every cry of my sick child pierced my heart, so I felt my cry was heard by Him whose love is stronger than even the love of a parent; for though a woman may forget her sucking child, our heavenly Parent will not forget us. I feel as if I can go up to town [to preach] with greater earnestness and zeal; feeling more the awfulness of sin, and at the same time realising more the tender compassion of a forgiving God."

And sister Ghetal recalls those sad times in these words: "It was after the death of my sister, that I was drawn into that closer relation with my mother which continued throughout her life. Having lost my little playfellow, she herself sought to be my companion, interesting herself in everything that gave me pleasure. Indeed, she desired to stand as far as possible in the light of a companion to all her children; and while she sought in some measure to interest our minds in those pursuits which chiefly engaged her attention, she entered cheerfully into everything which concerned us."[119]

---

[119] *Far above Rubies, Memoirs of H. S. H., by her Daughter.* Edited by R. H. Herschell, 1854

Chapter 23

So Deronda soon took his farewell for the two months during which he expected to be absent from London, and in a few days he was on his way with Sir Hugo and Lady Mallinger to Leubronn. He had fulfilled his intention of telling them about Mirah. The baronet was decidedly of opinion that the search for the mother and brother had better be let alone. Lady Mallinger was much interested in the poor girl, observing that there was a Society for the Conversion of the Jews, and that it was to be hoped Mirah would embrace Christianity; but perceiving that Sir Hugo looked at her with amusement, she concluded that she had said something foolish.

George Eliot, *Daniel Deronda*

Whether it was memories of daughter Esther at Edward Terrace or just the Victorian habit of moving from one rented home to another from time to time we may never know, but by June 1841 the Herschells had re-settled to the north of Chadwell Street Chapel in Gibson Square, Islington.

Ridley was planning a journey to Syria and Palestine with his young friend John Fuller-Maitland backed by another rich sponsor, and the work continued to prosper. Helen, as always, did her best to ensure that Ridley was not overburdened with worries about domestic affairs or finance. She was a trained musician and those who had heard her sing would not forget, "the sweetness of her clear, ringing voice, nor the exquisite taste and deep feeling with which she sang some of the glorious masterpieces of the great composers of sacred music."

So she began to give singing lessons on a daily basis in addition to the school work, her household responsibilities, the visiting programme and a hundred other tasks she had taken on as her share in the partnership. In the dark days which were to come for Ridley he would often recall tearfully the words from the book of Proverbs, "Who can find a virtuous woman? for her price is far above rubies."[120]

---

[120] Proverbs 31:10 (KJV)

About the same time Herschell began to investigate, with others, ways of bringing the Gospel to the Jewish people on a larger, more organised, scale. The London Society for Promoting Christianity among the Jews had been founded in 1809.[121] They needed workers and support, but its connection with the Anglican Church was, as ever, a problem for Ridley who saw a need for, "...the establishment of a society which should be unfettered by the formulas of any particular sect, and in which members of all denominations of Christians might join."

The poor old Church of England was, at least technically, a sect but the Nonconformist joint founders of the London Society had failed miserably to support them financially in building their first church for Hebrew Christians in 1814. They promised a £2,000 contribution, failed to raise the money and then withdrew from the plan entirely. Ecumenism, then as now, was a constant struggle with the commandment in John 13:34 that Christians should love one another.

A few years later, after a long and uncomfortable journey to Palestine, and feeling rather homesick, one of the first people Ridley visited was the new Anglican Bishop of Jerusalem, a Jew called Michael Solomon Alexander, from whom he received "the most Christian and friendly attentions during my stay in Jerusalem."[122] Ironically Michael Alexander was also the London Society's man in Jerusalem.

But it is likely the two men got on well together, though Michael was eight years older than Ridley. They came from the same Province in Poland, Poznań, and spoke the same languages, including Hebrew. Michael was an experienced Rabbi and had suffered many of the same doubts and struggles Ridley had gone through as he came to recognise the Messiah Jesus. The two scholars had much to agree on though Michael probably favoured separate missions to Jews and Gentiles. But, just like St. Peter and St. Paul, he would surely have agreed with Ridley's principal that: "There is not one truth for the

---

[121] In later years it would become The Church's Ministry Among Jewish People or simply CMJ

[122] *A Visit To My Fatherland*, Ridley H. Herschell, 1844

Jew and another for the Gentile, but as God himself is one and immutable, so is truth one and immutable. 'I believed, therefore have I spoken,' said the royal prophet; we also believe, and therefore speak. Could we believe these things and be silent?" "If Christianity be true, every Jew is bound to believe it as well as every Gentile. If Christianity be false, let Jew and Gentile alike denounce and reject it."

In 1842 Ridley helped to found the British Society for the Propagation of the Gospel among the Jews in spite of the fact that several similar organisations already existed. This was, after all, the golden age of societies. There were societies for the arts and science, societies for the protection of children and animals as well as endless Provident, Co-operative and Friendly Societies for the poor, and the long-established Royal Society for the Encouragement of Arts, Manufactures and Commerce, happily now known as the RSA.

But one of the most amusing came from Helen's own home town and described itself with deep Victorian benevolence as the Leith Female Society for Relieving Aged and Indigent Women. In 1823 the town also intriguingly boasted a Leith Auxiliary Society for Promoting Christianity Among the Jews, presided over by the Revd. Dr. Robertson. Any part Helen may have played in the Leith Auxiliary Society for Promoting Christianity Among the Jews is sadly lost to us. She is not mentioned in the records, perhaps because all the fifteen worthies, from the Directors to the Clerk and the Treasurer, were men.

Like many of these Victorian societies the British Society for the Propagation of the Gospel among the Jews itself is still working around the world today though it now goes under the more comfortable title of Christian Witness to Israel or CWI, and even in Victorian times was usually known as the British Jews Society.

7th of November 1842. A meeting to discuss plans for the British Jews Society was held in Edward Irving's old church, the Scotch Church in Regent Square[123], where, twenty years before, the ill-fated clergyman had preached to

---

[123] The National Scotch (or Caledonian) Church, Regent Square, London WC1, destroyed in World War II

congregations of two thousand. It was attended, according to Ridley's daughter Ghetal, "by ministers and laymen belonging to the Churches of England and, as well as to various dissenting bodies." It was also attended by the famous young preacher Robert Murray McCheyne[124] of Dundee who "offered a prayer at the opening." He had been preaching at a communion led by his friend the recently appointed Presbyterian minister, James Hamilton[125].

McCheyne had himself visited Palestine for health reasons in 1839 and may have inspired Herschell to make the long pilgrimage to his spiritual home in February 1843. Sadly, his own powerful and fruitful ministry in Scotland would be ended by his sudden death the following March, while Ridley was in the Holy Land. He was just twenty-nine.

Ridley would continue to support the British Jews Society for the rest of his life. He established a college for missionaries and would visit the mission stations around Europe to encourage them whenever he could. "He was one of the Society's staunchest friends and never-wearying labourers," wrote Mr B. Davidson, resident tutor at the college, "He was the soul of it."

Mr Davidson had also been involved with Ridley in the establishment of a Jews Benevolent Fund, "...with the view of alleviating the sufferings of destitute foreign Jews, and giving such aid to believing Jews as the means at command might render practicable."

Ghetal reports on the success of that operation: "In four years from that time, it was reported that seven individuals had been enabled to proceed to America, forty to return to the Continent, seventy-five had been assisted in business, and nearly five hundred had received casual aid. 'Some part of the fund for the relief of poor Jews' Mr Davidson writes, 'was confided to my charge, that by means of it I might also have opportunities for ministering to them in spiritual things. Mr Herschell induced Christian friends to supply me with clothing for men, women, and children of the poor among his people.'"

---

[124] Robert Murray McCheyne (1813-1843)

[125] James Hamilton (1814-1867)

Chapter 24

There is always more misery among the lower classes
than there is humanity in the higher.

Victor Hugo, *Les Misérables*

Israel Airlines flight Lima Yankee 216 leaves London every Friday for Tel
Aviv. It is the only El Al flight from Stansted Airport and it arrives in Israel
before the sun sets on Jerusalem. El Al doesn't fly on the Sabbath.

As the Boeing 737-758, *Ashkelon*, makes its steep descent to Ben Gurion
Airport the city of Tel Aviv-Yafo sparkles below in the early spring sunshine,
bright white, sprawling down the Mediterranean coast to the old port of Jaffa.

A five hour flight and an agreeable in-flight kosher meal brings us over the
tel aviv, the hill that Ridley would have seen from Jaffa when he first arrived, a
hundred and sixty years earlier in May 1843. Today Tel Aviv is home to nearly
400,000 souls. As Ridley travelled with his companion on the hard road from
Jerusalem to Jaffa, now the multi-lane Route 1 highway, Herschell saw a
glimpse of the future of that sadly neglected land which now blossomed
beneath us:

"On Tuesday, the 30th of May, we bade adieu to Jerusalem, and set out for
Jaffa, the ancient Joppa. About an hour after we left Jerusalem we were much
struck with the beautiful verdure of the trees in the orchards near which we
passed; a sight so rare in this land of drought and barrenness. Such spots
vividly call to mind what Palestine was, and what it will yet be."[126]

Ridley's own journey had begun two months earlier in Islington. It was
early Thursday morning, 9th February 1843. Black smoke from a thousand
ugly chimneys mingled with the fog on the nearby Thames to form a light but
bitterly cold, grey London smog. In spite of the weather many of the

---

[126] *A Visit To My Fatherland* , Ridley H. Herschell, 1844

congregation had turned out to see their Minister off from the Chapel in Chadwell Street. Young John Fuller-Maitland, Ridley's companion for the journey, who had made his way over from the comfort of Park Place, stood quietly by. Helen and the four children wrapped as best they could against the freezing fog had come down from the house in Gibson Square and prayed quietly with Ridley. This was no holiday trip. Ridley had already warned his congregation that he might not return from Syria, and Helen knew well enough the risks to a Jew travelling to Damascus at that time. It was still only three years since the notorious Damascus Affair, a blood libel which started with the disappearance of a Catholic priest and ended with a reign of terror involving the starvation of sixty Jewish children.

In 1840 The French consul in Damascus had accused the Jews of ritually murdering the priest in order to use his blood in religious ceremonies. The consul rounded up seven suspects and extracted a "confession" by torture during which one of the victims died. He then requested permission to kill the rest of his Jewish suspects. Other Jews, including sixty children, were arrested and starved in order to convince their parents to confess. No evidence whatsoever was ever produced and, thanks only to the intervention from England of Sir Moses Montefiore and others, the charges were finally dropped. But the terror lingered on and Damascus became a dangerous place for its 4,000 Jewish inhabitants. In A.D. 66, according to the historian Josephus, 10,000 Jews had been forced into the Stadium at Damascus and murdered. The Jewish people had long memories.

The coach was waiting at the Angel Inn, just a short walk from the chapel and would probably make the Dover connection at Welling. Tears were shed, clinging farewells were made and letters promised. Ridley and John boarded the gleaming stagecoach and it lurched into life with loud cries and the clatter of twenty-four iron hooves as they gripped the damp cobbled road. It pulled away with surprising speed and was soon engulfed in the swirling fog.

The journey from London to Paris via the Dover to Calais Channel crossing would take two days. It would be uncomfortable, exhausting, cold and probably dangerous. It would involve about twenty-four changes of the six horse team over the 283 mile trip. And that was just the beginning. After that would come Avignon, Nice and Genoa. If things went well they would reach Rome on the 18th February, nine days later. But this was as good as it would get in the heyday of coach travel. Soon the train would make the stagecoach a romantic memory, and that very year, 1843, the railway line from London to Folkstone would open. A year later the new track from Folkstone to Dover would be added and from there the steamship would whisk you to Boulogne, if the tide was in. A deep water port wouldn't exist in Boulogne until 1869. But the French railway from Paris hadn't yet reached the coast, so the stagecoach lived to fight another day, on the connecting route to Lille and the railways of northern France.

Ridley had last seen Paris in 1828 shortly before the brief Revolution of 1830 which would replace Charles X with the constitutional monarch Louis-Phillipe. Revolutionary France had been a monarchy again since 1814 when Louis XVIII became king following the Congress of Vienna and the apparent fall of the Emperor Napoleon.

Napoleon was to make a final comeback, only to be defeated once and for all at Waterloo in 1815, and Louis Phillipe would remain king until the peaceful declaration of the French Republic in 1848.

There had been many other changes in the French capital, and many more were to come. The Arc de Triomphe had been completed in 1836, crowning the Champs Élysée as the queen of tourist attractions for generations to come. The Impressionist painter Claude Monet had been born there in 1837 and the writer and reformer Émile Zola in 1840. But it would still be nearly fifty years before the Eiffel Tower would fix the popular image of Paris forever. For now, this was still the world of the forty-one year old Victor Hugo. The dreadful world of Jean Valjean and *Les Misérables*, which Hugo would immortalise in 1862, was never far away. And for Herschell the City of Light had now become a city of darkness: "Although in London we are too well used to the sight of vanity and sin, yet there is something in the ungodliness of Paris that cannot fail to strike one on entering it for the first time, or on returning to it after a long absence. You feel that you are 'where Satan's seat is;' and seem to behold the awful sight of a city wholly given over to the service of sin and folly."[127]

---

[127] *Ibid*

Chapter 25

O father Abram, what these Christians are,
Whose own hard dealings teaches them suspect
The thoughts of others!

William Shakespeare, *The Merchant of Venice*

We are not told what John thought of Paris. Younger brother of Esther Fuller-Maitland, he was a twenty-nine year old bachelor who would not marry for several years and the trip may have doubled as his Grand Tour. Certainly his future son, John Alexander Fuller-Maitland, writing in the late 1920s would describe it as such in his autobiography.[128]

But this was no ordinary Grand Tour, the culmination of a young man or woman's education. This was a whistle-stop trip through Europe, apparently missing out Venice and with no mention of the Pont du Gard or even Florence in Herschell's recollections.[129]

It is much more likely they were simply taking the scenic route to Palestine and both John and Ridley were aware of the altruistic and missionary nature of the journey. They would be visiting Jewish communities along the way and calling on mission representatives. If they could take in a few sights that would be a bonus. And if some members of the Maitland family, according to J.A. Fuller-Maitland, disapproved of or even despised the impoverished Herschell, it was not likely to have been John's parents, Ebenezer and Bethia. They could have sent John on a full-blown luxury tour any time and must have thought he could benefit from being with "the Rabbi". And anyway Ridley was funded, according to Ghetal Herschell, by Sir Culling Eardley, not the Fuller-Maitlands, or as Ghetal discretely puts it, "by whose kindness the journey was planned, and through whose liberality it was accomplished." And so the stop at Rome would include a visit which was never on polite society's Grand Tour itinerary,

---

[128] *A Door-Keeper of Music*, J.A. Fuller-Maitland, 1929

[129] *A Visit To My Fatherland* , Ridley H. Herschell, 1844

the horrific Jewish Ghetto.

The Ghetto, named after the Ghetto Veccio, the old Jewish quarter of Venice, which still has a lively Jewish community, was established in 1555 by Pope Paul IV. High walls were built with one main gate, and the Jews of Rome were put under a curfew. Any Jew found outside the walls at night could be punished severely. They were only allowed to work as tailors or trade in rags and second-hand goods. The Ghetto was seriously overcrowded and living conditions were appalling, even by the standards of the time.

When Herschell arrived in Rome the Ghetto was not the lively tourist attraction it is today[130], it was fully operational. He writes with uncharacteristic bitterness: "They (the Jews) live in a certain part of the city called the Ghetto, closed in by two gates, at each of which stands a sentinel; and so strictly are they confined to this place, that, when the Tiber overflowed many of their houses, a short time since, the sufferers were not allowed to move out of it, to obtain even temporary accommodation in another quarter. Close to one of the gates is a church,[131] on the outside of which is a representation of the crucifixion, under which there is written, in Hebrew, 'I have spread out my hands all the day unto a rebellious people.' [132] No Jew can go out or in by this great gate without beholding what he can only regard as a studied insult to his feelings. Did the Pope and his cardinals ever read the Epistle to the Romans, given forth by the Holy Ghost through Paul? "Boast not against the branches. But if thou boast, thou bearest not the root, but the root thee."[133] How wonderfully has professing Christendom overlooked God's oft-repeated declaration, that, though He punishes the Jews for their iniquity, He is 'sore displeased' with others who 'helped forward the affliction'!"

Another five years of suffering would pass before the Ghetto walls were

---

[130] The Old Ghetto incorporates the Great Synagogue and the newly renovated Jewish museum, the Museo Ebraico di Roma. It still has a thriving two thousand-year-old Jewish community.

[131] Santa Maria della Pietà, a short distance from the Jewish Museum.

[132] "I have spread out my hands all the day unto a rebellious people, which walketh in a way that was not good, after their own thoughts......"   Isaiah. 65:2. The inscription is there to this day.

[133] Romans 11:18

demolished when Italy became a republic. Full civil rights for Jews would have to wait until the country was united in 1870.

But in spite of everything Ridley was charmed by Rome as no doubt John was and every other visitor to the Eternal City has been. They visited St. Peter's basilica which Ridley grudgingly calls "a splendid edifice" but his comments on the hierarchy of the Roman Church as a whole were less than complimentary.

They no doubt saw the Sistine Chapel, the Trevi Fountain and the Spanish Steps and could hardly have missed the Coliseum and the Pantheon. But all these wonders are glossed over. They left Rome on March 30th after only twelve days. One day he would be back, but in very different circumstances.

By now they were travelling by diligence, a variety of stagecoach apparently inferior to the relatively sleek and sophisticated English mail coaches. By this and other more exotic means they made their way to Athens via the island of Corfu.

In Athens Herschell seems to feel more at home, perhaps away from the all-pervading religious influence of 'Rome' he had experienced through France and Italy. He stands on Mars Hill, where his beloved Paul had stood "before the wise and noble of Athens." Paul's words to the Athenians echo through his mind as he surveys the city: "God that made the world, and all things therein, seeing that He is Lord of heaven and earth, dwelleth not in temples made with hands."[134]

"It is impossible," writes Herschell, "to describe the vividness with which this address of Paul's came to my mind; and how very appropriate it is there felt to be. And if he stood there now, what could he say to the Athenians? Would he not still count them in all things 'too superstitious?' Would he not think their worship only a different form of idolatry; and declare that the God he served is still to them an 'unknown God?'"[135]

---

[134] Acts 17: 24

[135] *A Visit To My Fatherland* , Ridley H. Herschell, 1844

And at the Acropolis he was: "...overpowered by the scene; it surpassed anything I could have imagined. The labour and art which are displayed there, and the massiveness of the structures, all cry aloud, as it were, and declare the former glory of Athens."[136]

They left Athens "with much regret" and set sail for Smyrna (now Izmir, Turkey) arriving on 12th April. From Smyrna they were to take the steamer to Beirut in Lebanon, but it was delayed for more than a week and they took the opportunity to visit Constantinople, now Istanbul, in Turkey.

Finally, on Monday, the 24th April, "about three o'clock in the morning", having returned to Smyrna they set sail in an Austrian steamer for Beirut and the Middle East. By three that afternoon they were passing close to the island of Patmos where John, the author of the Gospel and the three letters bearing his name, had reported the words of Jesus to the seven churches in the *Revelation*. Herschell writes: "How many thoughts crowded on my mind as I gazed on this barren and desolate island! The wonderful vision vouchsafed to John, the chart of prophecy displayed to him, the awful and glorious things that 'shall be hereafter;' things still future, yet perhaps not far distant! Oh how speedily man's silly inventions and vain speculations fall before a believing view of 'the root and offspring of David, the bright and morning star!'"[137]

On Tuesday 25th April 1843 they landed on the island of Rhodes, then under Turkish sovereignty, which, Ridley observed, "the apostle Paul touched on his way from Ephesus to Jerusalem." And at noon on the 27th they arrived in Cyprus, also held at the time by Turkey, as it had been for nearly three hundred years, and once again they were in the footsteps of St. Paul.

Of Cyprus he writes ominously, and probably inaccurately, having met many fellow Jews in Rhodes a couple of days before, "There are no Jews in the island of Cyprus."

---

[136] *Ibid*

[137] *Ibid*

Chapter 26

"I will surely gather all of you, O Jacob;
I will surely bring together the remnant of Israel."
The Bible, Micah 2:12

Ridley and John finally reached Beirut on 28th April 1843. They had left the railways and the stagecoaches far behind them. In sixty years time the Wright Brothers would make their historic first powered flight at Kitty Hawk, North Carolina and in only another hundred years that Boeing 737 would fly us in armchair comfort to the Land of Israel. But from now on the journey for Herschell and young Fuller-Maitland would be by horseback, or on foot.

They reached the great city of Damascus in eight days. "A dirty, disagreeable place"[138], Herschell writes rather dismissively of the ancient capital in his journal, "We were now obliged", he complains, "to perform all our journeys on horseback; the roads in Syria, if roads they may be called, being quite unfit for carriages of any kind."[139]

It can be difficult to imagine in these times of demarcation, peace lines and precise but bitterly disputed borders, that the Turkish Ottoman Empire more or less prevailed all over Syria, Lebanon, Palestine and beyond. As in all great empires a fragile peace existed under its benevolent dictatorship and travel was fairly unrestricted for anybody foolish enough to undertake it. Ridley's companion even felt the need to carry a six-barrelled 'pepperbox' pistol which happily he never needed to use, except to show off to some impressionable Bedouin.

The standard of accommodation throughout much of the trip can be judged from Ridley's description of just one of their apartments:

---

[138] *Ibid*

[139] *Ibid*

"The room was so filled with the smoke of cow-dung (which when dried is used for fuel), that we could not see anything at a yard distant. After taking a little food, we spread our mats on the floor, and lay down to rest, as we fondly hoped; but, alas! no sooner had we settled ourselves, than such a fierce onset was commenced by the tiny inhabitants of the place, that all the previous assaults made on us, in Italy and elsewhere, were as nothing in comparison. In a little time I heard sundry strange noises in the room; and being unable to sleep, I got up, and took a light to examine what sort of companions we might have in the apartment that was professedly given up solely to our use. In one corner I found a calf; in another, a sick goat; over our heads, pigeons; and to complete the company, a cat with a litter of kittens. In the morning, when we were dressing, we were greatly annoyed by the women of the house, and some of their neighbours, coming to the door to look at the strangers; appearing quite unconscious that there was the slightest impropriety in their doing so."[140]

Whatever its shortcomings for Ridley, which included, it has to be said, the absence of a single Protestant church, he did make contact in Damascus with some of the large Jewish community whose hospitality they graciously received. During their three day stay they seem to have happily accepted the gratitude of middle class Jewish wives, their husbands being absent, on behalf of Sir Moses Montefiore who had intervened successfully in the dreadful blood libel of 1840!

The ladies, he tells us, with perhaps not a little impropriety himself: "...regaled us with coffee and sweetmeats, with the usual accompaniment of pipes, or nargilas. The nargila, which is like the Indian hookah, consists of a glass vessel full of water, that stands on the floor, through which the smoke is made to pass. It is inhaled through a long flexible tube having a mouthpiece. I was very awkward in the use of this machine (which it would have been esteemed very uncivil to decline), and could not get it to smoke at all, which one of the young ladies of the family perceiving, with a good-humoured smile at my awkwardness, took the mouthpiece out of my hand, and after two or

---

140 *Ibid*

three good whiffs, put it in smoking trim, and returned it to me."[141]

If we can believe royal biographer Lytton Strachey, Ridley's adopted Queen, Victoria, would certainly not have been amused:

"During her youth and middle age smoking had been forbidden in polite society, and so long as she lived she would not withdraw her anathema against it."[142]

Heading south out of Syria on horseback they finally entered modern Israel by a route unknown to most tourists. From the Damascus road they crossed the Jordon River by the Benot Ya'akov Bridge[143] from the Golan Heights just above the Sea of Galilee. Tradition says this was the route taken by Jacob on his return to Canaan after his northern exile from the wrath of Esau. From there Ridley says, they could see the Lake and even Tiberius in the distance.

As night was falling they made camp between the supposed sites of Bethsaida and Capernaum, not far from Korazin. Only in the 20th century would excavations uncover these long lost towns denounced by Jesus for failing to repent.[144]

The next day found them on the road to Tiberius along the banks of Lake Gennesaret, the Sea of Galilee. Suddenly, without warning, a storm blew up, as happens from time to time, and the peaceful lake became a real sea, foaming and crashing, making great waves as fearful as any salt sea. Then, as suddenly as it had started, the storm passed and there was silence again.

"We could quite understand the gospel narrative," Ridley reflects, "that when 'Jesus went into a ship with his disciples there came down a storm of wind on the lake; and they were filled with water, and were in jeopardy.'"[145]

---

[141] *Ibid*

[142] *Queen Victoria*, Lytton Strachey, 1921

[143] The bridge of the Daughters of Jacob

[144] Matthew 11:21-24

[145] Luke 13: 22, 23.

Tiberius today is a lively spa town glistening at night like a jewel on the beautiful lake that sometimes takes its name. Few worldly pleasures can compare to eating St. Peter's fish by Lake Tiberius on a warm summer's evening. But when Ridley and John arrived in the sacred city[146], named after the Roman emperor, it was in a sorry state. An earthquake in 1837 had all but destroyed it and the plague, in all its horror, had visited the city just two years before they arrived. Nearly a third of the Jews in the city had died. Most of those who remained were very poor and lived in tents. Everywhere they went Ridley was called upon to treat illness and disease. Their Jewish host in Tiberius was suffering from ophthalmia, a common eye disease which he treated, receiving grateful thanks from the man who had fully expected to go blind.

The story was the same throughout the land and in Damascus, Ridley believed, there was not a single medical man to be found. Back in England he called for all missions to have a medical person attached to them or that the mission worker himself be a doctor. The availability of simple medical treatment might also make way for the gospel where it might otherwise not be welcomed.

Their travels in the Land were clearly not without incident or even danger as this entry on the road to Samaria records:

"After resting about an hour we proceeded on our journey. Our ride was far from agreeable, as we met several rough and savage looking personages, armed with guns and spears. The country is in a very disturbed state; there is a constant warfare going on between the Bedouins and the Arabs."

But all the adventures and mishaps, all the joy and sadness experienced by Ridley and John, from ancient Damascus to Jerusalem, from the Sea of Galilee to the Negev Desert and the Dead Sea, would deepen beyond measure his love for the Jewish people and his belief in the restoration of Israel. He writes in his journal: "And now, having been permitted to behold the desolation of my fatherland, to witness its moral and physical degradation, what, it may be

---

[146] One of the four so-called sacred cities, Jerusalem, Hebron, Safed and Tiberius

asked, is the impression left on the mind? A feeling of hope and expectation, that as the night is so dark, the dawn must be near."

But, he continues, "the restoration of Israel is connected with the close of the Gentile dispensation. 'Jerusalem shall be trodden down of the Gentiles, until the times of the Gentiles be fulfilled.'[147] Whatever may be meant by the accomplishment of the times of the Gentiles, we may venture to say that it does not mean a time of outward ease, and worldly prosperity, such as many of the professing churches of Christ now enjoy; 'for then shall be great tribulation, such as was not since the beginning of the world to this time, no, nor ever shall be.'"[148]

"It is certainly a remarkable sign of the times", he writes after meeting Bishop Michael Solomon Alexander, "that a Jew should be sent out as bishop to Jerusalem by the most powerful nation of the earth."

The night was to get much darker. Perhaps the knowledge that the great tribulation to come might include the Holocaust, preceding the establishment of a Jewish homeland, would have been too much for Ridley to bear as he set off for England full of hope and expectation for his people.

Helen would be waiting, and the children. They were all well when he received their last letter in Jerusalem but now he wanted badly to see them and hold them again. Ghetal was now eleven years old, Mary was seven, Farrer six and Judah four. He would have to teach them about the Land and the people and the prophecies. He would take the boys to see it for themselves one day. And even later Farrer's youngest daughter Murial, at the age of sixty-five, would see the new State of Israel born out of blood and fire in 1948.

Back in Beirut they took a small sailing ship down to Alexandria and waited for the P & O paddle steamer to arrive. Writing a thank you letter to the American evangelist Eli Smith, their host back in Beirut, Herschell tells him: "About 2 o'clock the *Great Liverpool* arrived, by which I received good

---

[147] Luke 21:24.

[148] Matthew. 24:21.

news of the health of my beloved wife and children."[149]

There were no delays. To Herschell's great joy the *Indian Mail* steam packet had arrived on time allowing the *Great Liverpool* to sail for home. At 3 pm on Tuesday 20th June her tall twin smoke stacks billowing clouds of white smoke into the cloudless sky, the *Great Liverpool* paddle steamer left for England.

Stopping only at Gibraltar they arrived in Southampton three weeks later, 11th of July 1843. Herschell closed his journal with these lines: "after five months of pleasant association together, my esteemed fellow-traveller and myself had the happiness of again setting foot in England, his native, and my adopted, country, much gratified with having seen so many interesting places, and thankful for the gracious protection we had enjoyed in all our wanderings."[150]

---

[149] Eli Smith Family Papers, Yale University Library, Divinity Library Special Collections

[150] *A Visit To My Fatherland* , Ridley H. Herschell, 1844

Chapter 27

January 22. I don't generally lose my temper with servants; but I had to speak to Sarah rather sharply about a careless habit she has recently contracted by shaking the table-cloth, after removing the breakfast things, in a manner which causes all the crumbs to fall on the carpet, eventually to be trodden in. Sarah answered very rudely 'Oh, you are always complaining.' I replied: 'Indeed, I am not. I spoke to you last week about walking all over the drawing room carpet with a piece of yellow soap on the heel of your boot.' She said: 'And you're always grumbling about your breakfast.' I said 'No, I am not; but I feel perfectly justified in complaining that I never can get a hard-boiled egg. The moment I crack the shell it spurts all over the plate, and I have spoken to you at least fifty times about it.' She began to cry and make a scene; but fortunately my bus came by, so I had a good excuse for leaving her.

George and Weedon Grossmith, *The Diary of a Nobody*

Helen Herschell, age 46, mother of five children, four living, opened the front door of 60 Gibson Square, Islington and rested her hand lightly on the warm, black iron railings. The bright clear morning light prepared the comfortable Square for another perfect English summer's day. People passed by busily and, for a moment, invisibly in front of her as she paused.

"Good morning Mrs Herschell!" She smiled, and the gentlemen raised their hats and the tradesmen nodded respectfully. But it was all so far from the healing sun of the Galilee or the withering heat of the Judean desert. Did this adopted daughter of Zion dream of being there with Ridley in the Land, in Eretz-Israel, speaking Hebrew with the learned Rabbis, touching the stones that Jesus touched and breathing the air that carried the Messiah's words to an unbelieving world? Did her scholar's heart for a moment want to be in Alexandria where the P & O mail steamer waited under the clear Mediterranean skies of the ancient world's centre of learning? Perhaps she did, for an instant, but the words she had written in a very long letter to her sister twenty years before, just as the young Haim Herschell was planning his first visit to England, would have come back to her with gentle reproach: "But if those who wish to travel to Zion shrink from the difficulties of the way, they shall never reach it. Our Saviour nowhere promises an easy journey: - 'In the world ye shall have tribulations.' We are commanded to fight, to wrestle, to run; all implying active, and sometimes even painful exertion."[151]

This was where she was meant to be, with their children, discreetly supervising the chapel and, of course, the servants. Unlike poor Mr Pooter in The Diary of a Nobody Mrs Herschell probably didn't argue with Mary and Mary Ann, their two servants from the days in Brampton. Helen had, after all, successfully managed a large 19th century household for many years.

Mary Gray, the maid, a widow from Grafham, close to the picturesque Grafham Water, was thirty-one and Mary Ann Ellington, the cook from Brampton was just twenty-one. The excitement of being so close to London, at least for young Mary Ann, must have outweighed any fear of leaving their Huntingdonshire home, and we can only hope they were allowed by the Revd. Mr Herschell to occasionally go to the music hall on their days off. After all, this was not Paris.

As for the Chapel, it seems to have been left, in the absence of its Pastor, in the hands of somebody we can only identify as H.I.D. from a long and unauthorised introduction he wrote to the published version of Ridley's parting sermon. The sermon touched on the restoration of Israel and H.I.D. adds, perhaps a little pompously:

"The Writer of this address presumes that the Sermon itself will lose none of its interest by prefacing it with a few observations referring to the event anticipated; and he does this, not with the view of elucidating or supplying what may be considered deficient, but simply to make such statements more extensively known, and cause them to be more duly appreciated."

It is tempting to think that there may have been some conflict between H.I.D. and the substantial Mrs Herschell over the running of the church from time to time, but, alas, records have not been preserved.

And now Pastor Herschell himself was coming home. Helen knew he was booked on the 20th June sailing of the *Great Liverpool* but the ship could be delayed for up to five days if the mail from India was late and even without a

---

[151] *Far above Rubies, Memoirs of H. S. H., by her Daughter.* Edited by R. H. Herschell, 1854

delay the expected time from Alexandria to Southampton was two weeks. In this case it would be three, with a call at Gibraltar on 2nd July. Then probably on the new London and South Western Railway from Southampton to the South Western Railway Station at Waterloo. It would be a long wait, and she wouldn't tell the children quite yet, except perhaps Ghetal.

Chapter 28

We stopped to dine at Baltimore, and being now in Maryland, were waited on, for the first time, by slaves. The sensation of exacting any service from human creatures who are bought and sold, and being, for the time, a party as it were to their condition, is not an enviable one.

Charles Dickens, *American Notes for General Circulation*

From June 1843 to May 1846 Ridley and Helen would work together in Islington. During these years, in which Charles Dickens would publish *A Christmas Carol* and the 1844 *Factory Act* restricted young children to a mere six-and-a-half hour working day, the Herschells laboured among the poorest of the London poor, and the work grew as never before. From time to time Ridley would become restless and would travel, leaving the growing chapel congregation in capable hands and under the watchful eye of Helen. His heart was, as always, with the Jewish people and he longed to open what he called, "a home for Jewish inquirers into Christianity."

"Only one thing seemed to be wanting", wrote Ghetal, "greater scope for his labours among his Jewish brethren."

But there was little room for growth at Chadwell Street. The little chapel was hemmed in on either side, as it is today, by the three storey houses that slightly overlooked it and held it firmly between them like two burley Peelers.

One day, when Ridley was in west London, close to what would become Edgware Road Underground station, he noticed that a large livery stable was to be sold, a sure sign of the now rapid move to rail travel. Ridley didn't actually have any money, he never did, but he had acquired friends in high places, sometimes very high places. Such a friend was Sir Culling Eardley, great-grandson of financier Sir Sampson Gideon.[152] Sir Sampson himself was the son of a Portuguese Jew who had settled in London as a merchant of the West India trade, changing his name from Abudiente to the more convenient

---

[152] Sir Sampson Gideon (1699-1762)

and easily pronounced Gideon. Sampson, in his turn, changed the family name to the English sounding Eardley and Culling Eardley seems to have acquired the name Smith which he later dropped.

They had, at any rate, accumulated vast amounts of money between them and it fell to Culling, the re-invented English Christian gentleman and philanthropist, educated at Eton and Oxford, to give much of it away.

Sir Culling had already sponsored Ridley's trip to the Holy Land and Ridley, probably having no illusions about Sir Culling's roots, was keen to develop the relationship and further his ministry. Ridley invited his friend to buy the stables as a site for his new chapel and the Jewish home. Ghetal takes up the story: "Most generously and unexpectedly Sir Culling offered to procure the property, and thus the path was made a plain and comparatively easy one. Full of gratitude to God who had put it into the heart of one of His children to help him, he began with his usual energy to collect the necessary funds for building, and met with so much success and encouragement, that in April 1845 he felt himself justified in commencing operations, and the foundation stone of Trinity Chapel was laid."

Sir Culling, who seems to have been no mean operator himself, would make good use of Ridley's spiritual gifts in forwarding his own vision, the foundation of the Evangelical Alliance. On 10th August 1846, at a meeting of eight hundred delegates, representing fifty Protestant denominations, in the Freemasons' Hall, London,[153] Eardley's dream came true and the Evangelical Alliance was officially formed. Ridley made a lifelong commitment to the Alliance and it remains to this day the principal umbrella organization for evangelical Christians in the United Kingdom.

But before business could commence at the chapel Ridley had a major appointment in his diary. He had been invited to make a lecture tour in the United States by the American Society for Meliorating the Condition of the Jews.

---

[153] Freemasons' Hall was regarded as a neutral meeting place in 1846 and its use did not imply any endorsement of Freemasonry.

These were still adventurous times in America. At the height of the pioneering age, somewhere between the era of Daniel Boone and Davy Crockett but before the wild and woolly days of Wyatt Earp and Billy the Kid. The Big Country was getting bigger and still being carved up. Even while Herschell was there in 1846 the British and United States governments made an agreement on the status of Oregon, effectively controlled until then by the British Hudson Bay Company for the lucrative fur trade. Texas had been admitted to the Union the year before. The California Gold Rush was only a year or two away and the terrible Civil War and the abolition of slavery were still to come.

Into this world our hero arrived having left Liverpool on 19th April 1845 on board the *S.S. Hibernia* bound for Boston via Halifax, Nova Scotia.

It had been an eventful trip for the tri-masted steam paddle ship. With a maximum speed of nine knots and a wooden hull she had at one point been in serious danger of being crushed by icebergs. A contemporary report states:

"May 10, 1845: *SS Hibernia* at Boston reports encountered more ice on the Banks than the oldest fisherman ever saw before, was detained fifty-two hours, carried away part of the cutwater and nearly all the outer ends of her floats, bent the outer circles of her wheels, besides chafing her copper badly."

Another source had earlier reported several ships in trouble, including the *Hibernia*:

"May 6: Outward bound steamer *Hibernia* was seen by the schooner *Triumph* arrived here yesterday (Halifax) on Wednesday last (Apr 30) in 47° 30' W, about 250 miles from Cape Race steering to the southward to avoid the ice. Also: schooner *Ellen* lost on the seal fishery - Apr 27 150 miles to the westward of Cape Race after collision with an iceberg. Crew took to the ice and picked up later by the *St. John's Lass*."

The report concludes:

"The season of spring this year is unusually protracted .... owing no doubt to the immense barriers of ice by which our coasts are besieged, further to the eastward than the eye can extend. The arrivals from Britain are no doubt retarded solely by this cause."[154]

The *Hibernia* had accommodation for 120 first class passengers and, no doubt, many less privileged customers of the British & North American Royal Mail Steam Packet Company,[155] some perhaps on one way tickets to a new life or fleeing the potato famine in Ireland.

The fear had been so real that Herschell had invited some of his fellow passengers to join him for prayers for deliverance, and they did.

"During the period of suspense," records Ghetal with an appropriate sense of drama, "when the lives of all on board seemed in such imminent peril, he was thankful to be able to collect the passengers in the cabin, to direct their thoughts to the Father in heaven, who hears the cries of His children, and to join with them in earnest prayer that He would grant them deliverance. At length, to their great joy, the ship got clear of the ice, and the rest of the voyage was prosperously accomplished."

On his safe, if delayed, arrival he headed for New York and the Broome Street Church to celebrate the 25th anniversary[156] of his hosts, that is the American Society for Meliorating the Condition of the Jews.

The master plan of the Society's founder Elias Boudinot back in 1820 was to establish a "colony for converted Jews" in the New York area. When he died in 1821 he apparently left the Society 4,000 acres of land in Warren Co., Pennsylvania. Twenty-five years later, it seems, they still hadn't actually established the colony and had little prospect of achieving their founder's dream. They had sold the land in 1823 for a thousand dollars. A New York Newspaper, reporting the anniversary and, promoting Ridley to a Revd. Doctor for the occasion, reported the following: "The actual success of the Society in making converts does not appear to be very great. The receipts of the Society of the past year were $3716, of which $477 were received by

---

[154] National Research Council, Canada

[155] Later to be Cunard

[156] Founded 8th February 1820

132

legacies. The receipts show an increase of nearly double from those of the previous year. The Society publication, the *Jewish Chronicle*[157], has increased in circulation from 800 to 1300. The number of Auxiliary Societies formed during the year has been very encouraging, and much benefit is expected from their efforts.

Several distinguished scholars were present, and addresses were made by Rev. Dr. De Witt, Rev. Mr. Johns of Baltimore, and Rev. Dr. Herschell of England, who has just arrived in this country to prosecute his labors. The plan proposed by the Society to accomplish this object, is in the words of inspiration, 'to preach Christ crucified' and it is believed that the showing the simple history of the claims and evidences of its truth, and the zealous efforts of the various Christian churches, will accomplish the object of the Society - the conviction, and consequent melioration of the present Jewish nation."[158]

To what extent the Society eventually "ameliorated" the plight of the Jewish nation is not clear as they seem to have gone the way of so many worthy and optimistic organisations. But Herschell himself continued his tour of duty regardless of his own mixed feelings. The news of the death of his brother Joseph in Baltimore several years before his arrival had very much saddened Ridley and, writing home to Helen with the following summary of his punishing schedule, he shows a hint of his affection for her which touchingly breaks through his usual Victorian reserve. Baltimore was a long way from London in those days.

Tuesday 20th May 1845

I gave an address to a number of ladies who assembled at Mrs Mayor's, and I trust by the blessing of God the effort will be found a fruitful one in the cause of Israel; they seemed quite willing and ready to do something. In the evening I went to a party . . . The evening, I trust, was profitably spent. I expounded the Scriptures, and spoke faithfully to the company.

---

[157] No connection with the British newspaper of the same name

[158] Times and Seasons, Vol. VI No. 8 City of Nauvoo, Ill May 1, 1845

Wednesday 21st May at 4 p.m.

I met the Board of Directors again . . . I laid before them several important matters, which they adopted. I have therefore full confidence that a great and good work will be done for Israel in this country. In the evening, at half past seven, I gave a lecture to a large assembly; there were a great many Jews present. I was pleased to see one with his two daughters, who has followed me from church to church at every service.

Thursday 22nd May 1845

I was invited by the Bishops of the Episcopal Methodists to address the assembled clergymen who were present at the Conference. I suppose several hundreds were there. It was a very good opportunity of speaking to so many who are teachers of others. I spoke to them in the name of the Lord, and I found Him present with me to aid me in my endeavour to promote His glory.

Baltimore, Wednesday, 28th May 1845

On Sunday morning the 18th I preached to a crowded congregation at Dr Pottan's, at New York; a great number of Jews were present. In the evening I preached again to a congregation of about four thousand, and many were obliged to go away who could not get in. Many Jews were again present. Monday I felt very unwell and tired, but dined with Dr Pottan, to meet some of the leading men of the Christian Alliance. I hope some good will be done in this work. I have also addressed the Board of Directors of this Society, and have arranged to hold another meeting with them after my return from the South.

New York, Wednesday, 11th June 1845

From Baltimore I proceeded to a town called Wilmington, Delaware. I stayed in the house of a Baptist, a very good man . . . I preached to a large congregation in the evening, and had a public meeting the following morning, and then proceeded to Philadelphia. I preached three times on the Sunday, (June 1,) lectured again on Monday and Tuesday evenings, and had a public meeting on Wednesday. There was much interest excited. Many Jews came to my lectures, but I had no opportunity of seeing any to converse personally with them. I had also several calls from episcopal clergymen, who were anxious that I should preach to their flocks, but I had not time to stay longer. On Thursday morning I was invited by the Board of Directors of the Presbyterians, who are the representatives of the whole of that body, and have charge of their publications. The chairman stood up and addressed me in the name of the Board, thanking me for the service I have rendered them by the little book they have republished[159], and then presenting me with several books of their own publication. This was truly interesting, and a cause of great thankfulness. I left on Thursday the 6th inst. for New Brunswick, where I arrived late in the evening. Friday I was introduced to the Synod, and met a large body of the clergy. I had to address all these learned Rabbis in the evening; and a great many people assembled from all sects. I spoke for about two hours, and a very good impression was made. After the lecture, one of the members of the Synod proposed a vote of thanks to me for my very 'able and eloquent' lecture. I assure you, my beloved one, that my eloquence did not consist in speaking about flowers and stars, etc., but in a solemn appeal to their consciences. The Synod also resolved forthwith to take up the Jewish cause. Bless the Lord, O my soul, and forget not all His benefits.

Saturday 7th June 1845

I again arrived safely at New York . . . Sunday the 8th I preached in the morning to a very large congregation in a Presbyterian church. Much interest was excited. It was a plain gospel discourse. Dr Alexander, the pastor of the church, thanked me after the service, and said, 'This is the kind of preaching we want.' In the evening I was announced to preach in Dr Skinner's[160] church. It is a splendid place, and holds between two and three thousand people. It was crowded to excess. The subject was, 'The joy of the Gentiles dependent on the glory of Israel.'

---

[159] *A Brief Sketch of the Present State and Future Expectations of the Jews*, Ridley Haim Herschell, 1834
[160] Dolphus Skinner (1800-1869)

Wednesday 25th June 1845

I cannot tell you how very much I am refreshed and comforted by your letters . . . It is very hard work for me here; and I can only be sustained by the constant feeling that it is the work of the Lord, and that His glory must be my sole aim.

Chapter 29

"Be not afraid of greatness; some are born great, some achieve greatness, and others have greatness thrust upon them."
William Shakespeare, *Twelfth Night*

By the time he returned to England Ridley had become a respected and very popular Nonconformist minister. He had even published a collection of hymns in 1846 called *Psalms and Hymns for Congregational Worship* which would no doubt be used in his new chapel. And, since May 1844, he had edited the influential magazine *The Voice of Israel*. This was all in addition to his pastoral work, speaking engagements, travels among the Jewish people and writing several very popular books in his adopted language.

Ridley had long considered England to be his home and he had a great love for the country and its liberal traditions. It was, he often said, sometimes hard for the British to appreciate what they had as a nation. On his first journey to Palestine he had written home to the congregation at Chadwell Street: "I have not enjoyed a Sunday evening so much as this one since I left blessed England. I paced up and down the deck thinking of my dear congregation, and I joined with you all in spiritual worship."

Until 1844 it had required an Act of Parliament to become a subject of Ridley's "blessed England", but by 4th December 1845 the law had changed and he finally became a naturalized British subject. He was thirty-eight years old and soon to be Minister of a fashionable church in Marylebone. And he would finally get what he now called his home for wayfaring Jews, right next door.

"Though labouring equally for Jew and Gentile" wrote Helen, "he yet wished that his chapel should be a Jewish Mission Station, and expressed his desire that it might prove 'a little sanctuary to many of his brethren in the land of their dispersion.'"

The children were growing fast. Eldest son, Farrer, was now nearly ten. Many years later young Farrer would be remembered as: "playing about the streets in the neighbourhood of his father's church. He was a prominent figure at Bible-class meetings, and early displayed remarkable firmness and tenacity of purpose, and exceptional abilities."[161]

These exceptional abilities were to take Farrer far beyond the back streets of Marylebone. On his fifteenth birthday Helen, ever concerned not only for their education but for her children's spiritual growth and welfare, would write what might seem to us to be a rather formal letter to him at his private school:

"Many happy returns of this day to you, my darling boy. I cannot tell you with how much pleasure I now think of you, when I see that through the great mercy of God, as you are now approaching manhood, you desire to choose the better part that shall not be taken from you.

I can quite understand the diffidence and hesitation you may feel in making a public profession of your faith, from a dread that you should afterwards walk inconsistently. I would never recommend a premature profession, but it is not age that enables us to walk consistently, it is Divine grace alone, - Divine grace earnestly sought and carefully watched for. If you were twenty, you would be as dependent on this grace as you are now; and if the believer of sixty is unwatchful, he also will fall into sin. Be earnest, then, in prayer, my precious boy, and nothing can harm you. Cleave to the Church of God, and to the people of God; avoid, as the greatest danger, foolish and ungodly companions; and thus by prayer and watchfulness you will be kept from dishonouring Christ.

I was several years older than you when I first determined to leave all to follow Christ. I had mixed in the gaieties of a frivolous world, so I knew what I was giving up, and I can truly say I never for one moment repented of my choice, or looked back with regret on the world I had left; its pleasures and vanities were no more to me than the childish toys of my infancy.

God bless you, darling boy, and give you joy and peace in believing.

Ever your affectionate mother,

---

[161] Unidentified newspaper from Westminster Archives, dated 1899

H. S. Herschell"[162]

Helen's "precious boy" would keep his faith and would go on to achieve worldly fame through circumstances that could hardly have been imagined as Christmas 1845 approached. It would be their last Christmas with the much loved Chadwell Street congregation.

---

[162] *Far above Rubies, Memoirs of H. S. H., by her Daughter.* Edited by R. H. Herschell, 1854

Chapter 30

A town, such as London, where a man may wander for hours together without reaching the beginning of the end, without meeting the slightest hint which could lead to the inference that there is open country within reach, is a strange thing.

Friedrich Engels, *The Condition of the Working Class in England*

Success brought the Herschells new challenges, and new attacks. The foundation stone of Trinity Chapel had been laid by Sir Culling Eardley on Tuesday 8th April 1845. Daughter Ghetal reports: "A tent was provided for the accommodation of the spectators, but was far too small, for the whole neighbourhood seemed gathered together. Hundreds of the poor, who lived in the streets close by, were there to witness the commencement of a work which was by and by to bring a blessing into many of their homes. The day was exceptionally bright and sunny for the season, and its events have left a pleasing impression on all who shared in them."

Hopefully the residents of the nearby Christian Union Almshouses, still standing today, though in a very modernised form, joined in celebrating the arrival of their new neighbours across the road in John Street[163]. The celebrations may have relieved the misery of the lives of many local people for a day, but the spectre of hunger and poverty was never very far away, though west London did not seem to suffer the appalling conditions described by Engels in the East End: "I believe," said one of Engels' correspondents, "that till the Bishop of London called the attention of the public to the state of Bethnal Green, about as little was known at the West-end of the town of this most destitute parish as the wilds of Australia or the islands of the South Seas."[164]

But west London was much more than the "West-end" and Ghetal recalls,

---

[163] Now Crawford Place

[164] Mr. G. Alston, preacher of St. Philip's, Bethnal Green

probably from her own memory as an observant and intelligent teenager, "the streets immediately around were thickly populated with poor inhabitants." The Christian Union Almshouses, or to give them their full Victorian title, The Christian Union Almshouses for the Aged and Pious Poor in the North-West District of London, set a high standard of welfare for the time, "supported by voluntary contributions" of course, as it stated clearly beside the imposing front entrance.

Established in 1833 they were built to provide for "the reception of the poor and aged disciples of the Lord Jesus Christ", where, having reached the ripe old age of at least sixty, "in comparative peace and tranquillity, they might spend the remnant of their earthly pilgrimage, apart from the distressing trials to which persons are peculiarly exposed, whose poverty obliges them to live in a neighbourhood at once the abode of misery and vice."[165]

It is an indication of the extent of that misery in the outside world that the list of fourteen "Rules and Regulations" was so readily accepted by the fortunate few who were invited to live there. It included such cheerless, though not too onerous instructions, as:

5. The Inhabitants are expected to keep their rooms at all times clean and in decent order, being open to the visits of those benevolent Christians who have thus provided a comfortable home for their poorer brethren.

6. The Superintendents have authority to call at the several rooms at seasonable times; and it is expected that attention will be paid to any advice they may deem it necessary to give on the subject of these Regulations.

10. The wash-house may be used on every day but Saturday and Sunday. Each Inhabitant, beginning with No. 1, will be allowed the use of it for three hours: viz. from nine to twelve - from, twelve to three and from three to six; thus accommodating several persons each day. Each person, after using it, is expected to leave the place in decent order.

And, finally, a reminder that it would be another twenty years before the

---

[165] Westminster Archives, London

London Metropolitan Fire Brigade would be formed and paid for from the public purse. Until then the less than effective London Fire Engine Establishment, under the control of the big insurance companies, could not always be relied on:

14. Fires and candles must be carefully put out before 10 o'clock, in order to guard, under Divine Providence, against the awful calamity of fire. Should any exception be required in cases of sickness or other necessity, the Superintendent must be applied to for permission, who will furnish a safety lantern, to be expressly used on the occasion.[166]

A little over a year later, on the Wednesday 27th May 1846, the chapel was finally opened for worship. It could accommodate 1,200 people and the Terms of Membership, according to Charles Dickens' son in his *Dictionary of London* were "a profession of faith and believer's baptism."[167]

Above all there were many Jewish people living in the area. After the first morning service with the independent minister Dr John Leifchild[168] and several others assisting, the afternoon service was conducted entirely by Christian Jews with a sermon by Ridley.

A century and-a-half later, amid the multicultural bustle of twenty first century London, where Arabic has long replaced Yiddish as the main immigrant language and *Caffè Latte* has almost replaced the traditional cup of tea, I stood outside Trinity Chapel and listened for an echo of that first sermon. The traffic is very much quieter now, no clatter of horseshoes or rumble of cartwheels, just the hum of hi-tech buses and the entomological buzz of scooters picking there way through the slow moving cars.

Trinity Chapel itself has all but gone too, converted to a synagogue in 1961, it was changed almost beyond recognition. There was, wrote the author

---

[166] *Ibid*

[167] Baptism, often involving full-immersion in water, of a consenting and believing person as opposed to, or in addition to, infant baptism of a child who has not made a personal faith decision..

[168] John Leifchild (1780-1862)

of a history of the Western Synagogue[169] with reference to Herschell's Messianic magazine *The Voice of Israel*, "a certain poetic justice in the fact that within this new building there was now to resound a very different Voice of Israel and that it was to become the centre of the propagation of Judaism to the Jews."

But sadly all good things come to an end and by the early nineteen-nineties the Western Synagogue had moved once again and been amalgamated with the Marble Arch Synagogue in Great Cumberland Place. This beautifully understated modern building lying behind its imitation Regency colonnade can accommodate a thousand worshippers. In addition, on the first floor, is the Minz Beth Hamidrash, a much smaller synagogue surrounded by artificially lit framed stained glass.

Outside, in a square just across the road, is a statue of Holocaust rescuer Raoul Wallenberg, the Gentile Swedish businessman and diplomat who helped to save about 100,000 Jews from the Nazis. He is surrounded by a representation of the 20,000 Swedish passports he is said to have issued to Jewish victims.

In 1945, at the end of the war, Wallenberg was imprisoned by the Soviets and is believed to have died in a Russian prison in 1947.

Back at Crawford Place the new building, like some battered Crusader castle, is again in the hands of the Christians, and the Seventh Day Adventist Church now meet there every week on the Jewish Sabbath. The whole beautiful irony would not have been lost on Ridley as he settled into their new home at 36 Newnham Street just round the corner from the chapel.[170]

And Ridley's first sermon at Crawford Place? Sadly the echo had long died away and, since Herschell preached with very brief notes which were placed in the Bible he always held in his hand while preaching, we may never know what he said. But we can be sure, as Ghetal tells us: "His text was generally a

---

[169] Arthur Barnett, *The Western Synagogue Through Two Centuries 1761-1961*, 1961

[170] Now Brendon Street

passage of Scripture containing a complete subject - sometimes one, some-times several verses, a whole parable, a narrative, a biography, or a statement of some Christian doctrine. This he would thoroughly think out for himself, endeavouring to enter into the spirit of the time in which the words were spoken, and of the people by whom and to whom they were uttered; looking at the obvious meaning which appeared on the face of the words, or seeking to bring to light what seemed obscure; always trying to be himself satisfied with the explanation which he intended to put before his people. He did not, despise the labours of commentators, but he was never content to adopt their opinions unless after much thought and study he had made them his own." His friend T.R. Wheatley, who belonged to his church for many years wrote: "His sermons were a kind of expansion of himself, he did not preach so much as think aloud in the pulpit."

That may have been the impression he gave, but Ridley would actually spend Friday and Saturday morning preparing his work for Sunday and was much influenced by the Revd. Richard Cecil[171] on the subject of sermon preparation: "I was cured of expecting the Spirit's influence without due preparation", wrote Cecil, "by observing how men talked who took up that sentiment. I have heard men talk nonsense by the hour, as 'the Spirit enabled them.'" But Ridley rarely used his notes on the day as he was "so thoroughly acquainted with the Bible, that he could quote passage after passage from memory." Here is part of a sermon given at Chadwell Street three years before on Hebrews 11:16 which was taken down in shorthand.[172] The Revd. Herschell, frock-coated, he would never wear a gown in his own chapel, stands in the high pulpit before a packed congregation. Bible in hand, his steady, gentle eyes seeming to make contact with every individual who had the courage to look at him, he begins to speak, slowly, carefully, to the "unconverted":

"But now they desire a better country, that is, an heavenly: wherefore God

---

[171] Richard Cecil (1799-1865)

[172] Probably the recently devised Pitman Shorthand of Sir Isaac Pitman (1813-1897) first published in 1837.

is not ashamed to be called their God: for he hath prepared for them a city."
Hebrews 11:16.

"I now address myself to the unconverted - and may God give me grace to speak solemnly, affectionately, and faithfully. Take this subject, and ask your own souls, Do you desire a better country, that is, an heavenly? and, if you are honest, your answer will be, No, we do not; we are satisfied with earth; we labour for it; we know it: it affects our senses; it suits our feelings: we know an earthly country, but as for that which is heavenly, we look not for it. And if I ask again, Do you not then expect to be miserable in eternity? You reply, Oh, no! God cannot be so unmerciful: we cannot help ourselves; we are placed in such a position, and what are we to do? He will not cast us away; I dare say we shall be saved. Ah, my dear friends, how can I say to you that God is not ashamed to be called your God? you, who believe not upon Him; who only make mention of His mercy as a cloak for your sin. You speak of His mercy -- but to what purpose? Is it because you wish to love, honour, serve, and obey Him? or is it not rather, because you despise Him in your heart, and yet imagine that it would be cruelty in Him to cast you away? You deny the character and attributes of God as a just God. You would wish Him to be such an one as yourselves, who would conform exactly with your desires; a deity before whose shrine you could bow and say, this is the god I love to worship. But when the true and holy Being appears; when He manifests Himself in the Son of His love; when He speaks to us by the sighs, the groans, the tears, the sorrows, the death, and the resurrection of Jesus, you despise Him in your hearts, although you may pay some sort of verbal homage to Him. I appeal to your hearts and consciences, and ask you in the sight of the living God, is He in all your thoughts? Do you seek to honour Him in all your ways, or even in any of your ways? Is it at all the desire of your heart that you may be happy in His presence? Can you say, that God is your God?

You cannot, you dare not. You may speak of His benevolence, and say, He will not cast me into outer darkness, although He has plainly threatened it in His word. You may say this; but it is not from your inmost soul; you cannot say that you positively expect to be happy in the presence of God. You may sneer at, and speak of persons who are what you term 'over-religious,' as fools: but if they have believed in the Redeemer, and look unto the cross alone for their salvation, you may call them fools, but they are truly wise, and shall shine forth as stars in the firmament of heaven, while you find out your own folly when it is too late; and this will aggravate your woe, for the recollection that it is your own folly which has urged you on, will add indescribable bitterness to your misery. My dear friends, can you say, that God hath provided a city for you? Or can you say, that God himself has raised up blessed mansions, into which you shall enter? Oh, alas, no! It is indeed true, that these mansions are prepared -- and the everlasting doors have been thrown open -- many have entered, and yet many more shall enter in and praise His name. ...Dear friends, is it not then quite clear, that in your present unholy and unregenerate state you cannot expect to enter into that city? And is it to be thus with you to the end? Are the doors to be for ever shut against you? You now hear the voice of a brother and a friend addressing you, and saying, 'Believe in the Lord Jesus Christ, and thou shalt be saved:' and then shalt thou be welcomed within that city by the happy beings who are there, and they will receive you into their brotherhood and fellowship! But what is awaiting you if you continue to despise these mercies? The Bible tells us, and your own consciences will tell you, that if you despise this proffered mercy, there remaineth nothing but a fearful looking for of wrath and fiery indignation."[173]

Herschell was a rare preacher in any generation.

---

[173] *The National Restoration of the Jews to their Fatherland, and Consequent Fulfilment of the Promise to the Patriachs.* A sermon delivered on Sunday evening, February 5, 1843, at Chadwell Street Chapel, Islington, by the Rev. R.H. Herschell, previous to his departure on a mission to Syria and the East. 1843, Jackson and Walford, St. Paul's Churchyard.

Chapter 31

And did the Countenance Divine
Shine forth upon our clouded hills?
And was Jerusalem builded here
Among these dark satanic mills?

William Blake (1757-1827)

The seven years from 1846 to 1853 were to be very special to Ridley and Helen. Not only would they find their place in the world, confident now of God's direction for them, it would also be their last seven years together.

Helen had worked tirelessly from the start of their ministry, not only to support her husband's work and raise a family, but in using her own evangelistic gifts. Once they had moved into the new home in Newnham Street, next to Trinity Chapel, and established the "home for wayfaring Jews" close by, she began what must have been a desperate race against failing health.

Her first task at Trinity was to set up the Sunday School. Not, as we might be tempted to think, a busy but enjoyable hour with the church children playing with sandpit models of Bethlehem and reading Bible stories together. This was a real school, and Sunday was the only day most children in the area could attend.

Children could still be made to work for up to six-and-half hours a day, and that was only the legal limit. Sunday was, more often than not, the only day of rest for working-class families and their children. So it was also the only day to acquire the minimum literacy and numeracy skills required to work in the new industrial society.

Helen Herschell was a very good teacher. She seems to have been way ahead of most of her contemporaries in believing that education should be a pleasure, not just a chore. She was, of course, just as committed to her own children's' education.

"It was always my mother's aim," her eldest daughter writes, "to make us love study for its own sake, and she always impressed upon our minds the truth, that the amount of lessons got off by heart would not benefit us, unless we adopted the facts or principles contained therein, and made them our own. "What new ideas have you gained today?" she would often ask with a smile. She wished to see us all fond of reading, and anxious to make progress in our studies, and afforded us every opportunity for that purpose, thinking it worth while to make any sacrifice for the education of her children."

The ravenous needs of industry for a numerate and literate workforce would set the pattern of education in England for a hundred years to come, but any child taught by Mrs Herschell or her staff would learn much more than spelling and tables. A major event in the life of the school is related by Ghetal many years later, reminding her readers of the ghetto-like conditions of the working-class during her own childhood: "In the summer of 1850, through the kindness of Mr Wilbraham Taylor, permission was obtained from the late Prince Consort to take the school children and their parents to spend a day in Windsor Park. This expedition was planned before such excursions were as common as they now are, and it seemed rather a formidable undertaking. But nothing could be more successful. The day was most favourable, and Mr Herschell and the many friends who accompanied him were made happy by witnessing the delight of the children in their gambols on the greensward under the shade of the trees, with the bright blue sky overhead, and the sun shedding a glory upon all - a delight unknown in the midst of courts and alleys - and at that time a greater novelty to many of those enjoying it than it would be now."

Ghetal may be idealising the trip just a little but the contrast was very real between the wide open spaces of Windsor and the dark oppressive maize that was home to most of the children.

Next came the District Visiting Society, high on the wish-list of any philanthropic Victorian lady with a heart for the poor and needy. Visitors would be sent out into the community to seek and comfort the sick, encourage children to join the Sunday School, perhaps teach some basic hygiene or household management and, most importantly, bring to the attention of the clergy, or in this case Mrs Herschell, the pastoral needs of the parish.

One place the Society would not need to visit was the London home of the Fuller-Maitlands, just round the corner in Bryanston Square. This is an area where a ground floor apartment in a five storey house can command a rent of £1,500 ($2,750) a week today. In the mid-nineteenth century the Fuller-Maitlands owned a whole five floors and probably only used the house during the twelve week "London Season".

Eldest daughter Esther Fuller-Maitland had kept in touch with the Herschells and may have been the one who brought the Chapel site to Ridley's attention. Unmarried and now in her forties the strong-willed, short-sighted Esther was said to have lost the hand of a marquis at some time as the result of a letter going astray in the post. Other offers of marriage had evidently not been forthcoming, or had been rejected by the popular maiden-aunt.

Ridley and Helen grew closer in their lives and their ministry. Between their very rich friends on one side and their often very poor parishioners on the other, they set to work. In spite of his struggle against service in the Church of Scotland and his early conviction that he was not called to ordination in the Anglican Communion, every step of his journey, from Leigh and Brampton, to Lothbury and Islington, showed him that he had been called to the duties of a pastor. And as Ghetal writes of these happy years, "there is of necessity less to narrate concerning them, as his duties did not differ from those of other Christian ministers." And so the years passed. The boys were sent to school in Camberwell Green[174], as boarders, but not too far away in what was then a Surrey village. The girls studied under Helen. The world changed even more rapidly than it had for the first fifty years of the century. The Great Exhibition of 1851 in Hyde Park, promoting the new technology of the time, came and went, as did its six million visitors, and western civilisation stumbled towards the brave new world of Nietzsche and Freud, Darwin and Huxley. But Ridley Herschell preached the same Gospel of salvation to rich and poor alike, and just as the fishermen of Leigh did, many more responded to the call.

---

[174] David Fletcher & Son's Grammar School, Denmark Hill, Camberwell

Chapter 32

Good-night, good-night! Parting is such sweet sorrow
That I shall say goodnight till it be morrow.

William Shakespeare, *Romeo and Juliet*

The University of Bonn, or to give its full and very official German title, *Rheinische Friedrich-Wilhelms-Universität zu Bonn am Rhein*, was founded in 1818. Today it is the largest university in Germany. And it seems, just as today, a good education was cheaper in Germany than in England. So, as both Ridley and Helen spoke fluent German and had brought the children up to speak it too, it made sense to send Farrer and Ridley Judah to Bonn for their further education. University was not an option for Ghetal or Mary at that time, but Helen had educated Ghetal and would teach Mary too, in spite of the social restrictions. And it gave Helen a chance to do some occasional travelling in her own right.

It was now the fall of 1853. The great city of Bonn, the future capital of a divided Germany, sat comfortably secluded in the Rhine Valley awaiting her destiny. One by one the gilded brown leaves gave up the struggle to survive and drifted slowly and randomly down to the murmuring Rhine, swirling their way through the Münsterplatz and around the new Beethoven statue. It was, Ghetal recalled, "...a glorious autumnal Sunday, when the sun was shining in full splendour. In a little upper room, in a strange land, where the name of God is not honoured, a few of His children were gathered together to celebrate His praise."[175]

Just ten people made up the little congregation that Sunday morning in Bonn, including the Herschell family. There were Ridley and eldest son Farrer, now sixteen. And there were the girls, Ghetal, married in August to

---

[175] *Far above Rubies, Memoirs of H. S. H., by her Daughter.* Edited by R. H. Herschell, 1854

physiologist John-Scott Burdon-Sanderson and Mary, mature and sensible at seventeen. Then there was the youngest, Ridley Judah, just fourteen. And, of course, Helen, tired and weak from her recent illness but joyful to have seen her daughter married, in answer to her prayers, to a God-fearing man.

They had all left for Germany shortly after the wedding at Trinity Chapel, the whole family; Ghetal and John on their honeymoon, Farrer and Ridley Judah off to college and Mary to stay with her mother in Bonn for the winter. The little service in the upper room some weeks later seemed a treasured opportunity for the family to be all together, perhaps for the last time, away from the busy life in London.

The next day Ridley, Ghetal and John would return to England. Helen had insisted on remaining in Bonn in spite of her poor health. She could not leave her sons to what she called, "the temptations of a German university.[176]" She had not planned to return until March 1854. At the end of September, on their wedding anniversary, she wrote home optimistically to Ridley: "I assure you, if you feel your strangeness at home, I feel my exile from you no less. I look upon the whole as a sacrifice we are called on to make for the good of our children; and think it will soon pass away, and we shall be restored to each other, not again to be so long separated. I have no doubt you thought of me to-day," she continues, "and of this day twenty-two years. With what thankfulness can we look back on all the way whereby the Lord has led us! If we could twenty-two years ago have seen ourselves in our present position, how delighted should we have been!"[177]

But in October she confided to Ghetal that she had not been well enough even to read: "Papa speaks of the monotony of our life here, but this is never disagreeable to me; that is, I do not mind monotony from without, if I can have my own private changes. I am thankful to say I have begun to read within the last few days."[178]

---

[176] *Ibid*

[177] *Ibid*

[178] *Ibid*

Ridley knew already that Helen was no longer taking her daily walks and this had concerned him greatly. In London she had always managed to walk up to Regent's Park, though stopping frequently on the way to rest with her book. But not to be able to read from time to time was a very serious development.

Early in November Ridley left again for Bonn, this time determined to bring Helen back home. But he arrived to find her in good spirits and, according to Ghetal, "my mother seemed revived before he left, and we all hoped that the remedies she was taking were beginning to benefit her."[179] Needless to say, he failed to persuade her to return to London and Ghetal records: "She resolutely decided on remaining where she was, saying that the climate was not hurtful to her, and it would be a great pity to disturb the children in their studies."[180]

Ridley knew, after twenty-two years, that she would not give in. She had never turned back since leaving Scotland to marry this gentle Polish Jew, and she was not going to change now. Ridley whispered instructions to Mary as he left. She must write to him immediately if thing got worse and he would come back. Mary kissed him and said she understood. He knew she did.

Back in London and alone now in what seemed such a large and silent house Haim Herschell finished his work for the day and started to write with a faltering hand to the wife put aside for him that day in Paris when Messiah Jesus called him. He knew in his heart that the same Messiah was now calling her home.

The single gas light on the corner of Newnham and John Street had been lit while he sat at his desk. The letter he had written now slipped from his hand as the long, dark winter night overtook him. Ridley slept.

My own darling wife,

My heart and mind and all my best feelings have been directed to heaven

---

[179] *Ibid*

[180] *Ibid*

in prayer and thanksgiving for you, my precious one. As soon as it was light enough to read, I took your large Bible into bed, and began to search out the passages of Scripture you had marked from August 1831 and onwards. Oh, how it recalled to my mind past times; how wonderfully has God dealt with us; what a remarkable history has ours been from our first meeting to the present day! We can sing of the mercy of the Lord, and shout His praises. I have no doubt you are to-day thinking, as I am, on the past goodness of the Lord. How I long to talk with you to-day, and how my heart is pained when I think that I left you so feeble and poorly . . . God bless and spare you, and grant that we may be permitted to spend many happy years together, to watch over our children, and glorify our Lord!

Your own attached

Ridley

More letters now passed between them as the distance seemed to bring them even closer. On Wednesday, 21st December, Helen wrote home to say she felt much better than she had done for some time. Ridley was pleased. The letter arrived on the Saturday and yet another one the following Monday, Boxing Day. The dark German stamp stood out clearly from the Penny Reds on the usual inland mail. But this one wasn't from Helen. It was from Mary. He opened it slowly, reluctantly. "Dear Papa......" He knew before he read it that the news was not good. Mary would not have written otherwise. Helen would write the good news. So the call had come at last, Helen was seriously ill. He summoned Ghetal and son-in-law John and they set out almost immediately for the Channel and Germany.

It was bitterly cold and confusion with train connections at Mechelen[181] in Belgium made the long journey even more horrendous than it might have been. They arrived in Bonn, freezing and tired, on the evening of 28th December instead of the early morning. Ridley went straight upstairs to see Helen. Ghetal and John crouched around a recently lit stove for some warmth.

---

[181] Malines

As he entered the room the children's faces turned to him expectantly. Papa was a doctor. Surely he would know what to do. Ridley looked down at his wife. She had changed so much in so short a time.

"Your mother is very, very ill," he said, trying to appear professional and detached, and then added quietly, "Children, I ought not to conceal it from you; God can do all things, but, humanly speaking, there is no hope of her recovery!"[182]

On the 29th they took it in turns to sit with her. She drifted in and out of consciousness and from time to time spoke of her concerns for the family and the missed Christmas celebrations. She even arranged meal breaks for them; "It is your dinner hour now," she said to one of the children, "you must not stay here" Ghetal, who stayed with her mother most of the time anyway, takes up the story:

"On the morning of the 30th my mother was very weak. Her sight and hearing were much impaired, and she often appeared quite unconscious of what was passing around her. We all assembled by the side of her bed, and my father prayed aloud that God would continue with her to the close, and would sustain and comfort us. Then going close to my mother, he said, "The Good Shepherd will not leave you, He will be with you to the end." A smile, more of heaven than earth, overspread her face on hearing this, and when my father asked, "Do you feel the Good Shepherd near you?" she answered distinctly, "Yes." She had almost lost the power of speech. My father said once more, "Good bye, my darling wife, goodbye," and then her lips moved "Goodbye," though we heard no sound. She seemed then really to have bid farewell to earthly things, and was, to all appearance, unconscious the greater part of the day. Once she said, "my dear children," and appeared to have a pleasing recollection of the interview in the morning; once, when her lips were moving, the name of God was distinguished, doubtless in prayer. She seemed conscious of my father's presence to the last, for, on the evening before her death, when he went to the bedside. She turned round her face towards him, though she

---

[182] *Far above Rubies, Memoirs of H. S. H., by her Daughter.* Edited by R. H. Herschell, 1854

gave no sign of recognition when any one else approached her. On the morning of the last day of the year we were all standing near the bed. My mother lay there with a calm and peaceful look. She did not seem to suffer at all; God graciously spared herself and others from this additional pain. She was breathing very quietly, and at intervals, till, at half-past seven o'clock, one gentle sigh was heard, and all was over!"[183]

Helen died as she had lived, close to her family and her Saviour, but the new year of 1854 arrived without celebration from the little family. The formalities dealt with, swiftly and efficiently in the German manner, Ridley, Farrer and Ridley Judah accompanied Helen's body on the long painful journey to London. One day Farrer himself would be carried home to England, from America, on board the Royal Navy frigate *HMS Talbot,* to be met at Portsmouth by a funeral guard of a hundred sailors and a hundred Marines for his own funeral service at Westminster Abbey. But that was still to come for the eldest son of Ridley and Helen. The new year of 1854 had arrived without ceremony and without joy for the future Lord Herschell.

Mary had already gone ahead with John and Ghetal. The men had stopped in Cologne to change trains and rest. Ridley Judah, confused and alone in his room writes to his older sister Mary as he has so many times before:-

Cologne, January 3, 1854.

My Very Dearest Mary,

How little we thought that before this day our beloved mamma would be in heaven singing praises to God! It is a sore affliction; but we see God's hand ruling all - how everything was ordered by Him. O Mary! God gave us this affliction for some cause. He never gives pain for no reason. Oh, we ought to strive to enter in at the strait gate, to avoid Satan's temptations, and to love God with all our hearts. O Mary! let us strive from this day to go on together - every day feeling we are nearer to God than the day before; if we do this we

---

[183] *Ibid*

shall be very happy. But oh, it is difficult - so very difficult - to keep in the right path! We must help one another, and try to do so in every way, constantly seeking grace of God.

I remain your loving brother,
Ridley.

Ghetal too recalled a life so suddenly taken away from them, never to return:

"Among the times which dwell with most sunny brightness on the memory are the Sunday evenings, when, after the various occupations of the day, the whole family assembled together, the young ones so full of gaiety and mirth that the mother would at length say, half in fun, half in earnest, affecting the Scotch accent, which she had almost entirely lost, "Children, what would folks say to this noise and laughter in the minister's family on the Sabbath night!" She only wished, however, to moderate, and not to check it; for she believed that youthful spirits must have vent, and that the somewhat undue exuberance on the Sunday evening was a consequence of the restraint put upon themselves in the previous part of the day; and she considered it far better that the natural joyousness of childhood and youth should have free play in harmless mirth in the presence of the parents, than be so kept down that it should burst forth in a more objectionable way when beyond parental control. It must not be supposed, however, that rebuke and punishment were withheld when necessary; but these were almost entirely kept for transgressions of the moral law - untruthfulness, disobedience, self-will, and the like - and not for mere childish failings, irregularities of outward conduct, or other offences not involving the principles of right and wrong in God's sight."

They all arrived back in London as the 1853-54 cholera epidemic was claiming its last victims. 10,738 had died. It was bitterly cold and the ground was hard as stone at Kensall Green Cemetery where Helen was laid to rest. The funeral service took place in the sober Nonconformist Chapel on Thursday 12th January 1854. Helen was buried close to the Regent's Canal in a grave deep enough to hold several members of her family, but no one else would ever be buried there. The Herschells were only to be reunited in that heavenly country of Hebrews 11:16.

Ridley was not fond of writing letters but he was a man of his time and would write in an affectionate but quite formal style even to his young children. After all, his letters could have been opened by school staff or read by fellow pupils and he needed to comply with Victorian etiquette in his adopted language.

But a private letter, written from Palestine in 1843 and gathering dust in a University library[184] where Ridley could never have imagined it would end up, gives his wife her full and personal title. To Haim Herschell she would always be, "My darling and tenderly beloved Helen."

---

[184] University College London

Chapter 33

Winter is come and gone,

But grief returns with the revolving year.

Percy Bysshe Shelley, *Adonais: An Elegy on the Death of John Keats*

Esther Fuller-Maitland, near neighbour and old friend of the Herschells, had, it seems, become a perpetual aunt since the days at Park Place. Esther had found that being an aunt, like being a grandparent, had many of the benefits of parenthood with few of the drawbacks.

Her early brush with matrimony seems to have convinced her that being a favourite maiden aunt was to be her role in life, and she fulfilled it admirably as far as the children of her elder brothers and sisters were concerned. The children of her younger siblings were, according to niece and one time music critic of *The Times* John Alexander Fuller-Maitland, rather less favoured.[185]

Aunt Etty, as she was known to those children who were devoted to her, lived just half a mile from Trinity Chapel, at 28 Westbourne Terrace, the fashionable end of a very mixed West London community. Even fifty years later, at the turn of the century, the *Marylebone Mercury* could describe the chapel's environment as "almost unique": "for the neighbourhood in which it stands is inhabited by the very wealthy and by the very poor. To the west of the chapel are the great commercial houses of Edgware-road: and further beyond the palatial residences of the leaders of fashion and society. On the east and south are the overcrowded tenements of the toilers and the little shops of struggling tradesmen. On the one side, riches and luxury; on the other, poverty and busy toil."

How much worse things must have been in 1854 can hardly be imagined.

---

[185] J.A. Fuller-Maitland, A Door-keeper of Music, 1929

With the horrors of typhus and cholera not yet under control[186] few people among the London poor at that time would live beyond forty years, and even the highest in the land could not escape the fatal clutches of typhoid fever. In 1861 Queen Victoria's beloved Consort, Prince Albert, fell victim to the awful disease at the age of forty-two.

Although the Queen went into full mourning for three years, taking her court with her, the generally accepted period was just two years, with some relief for women with children who needed to re-marry and some further discretion for men.

Ridley Herschell would formally mourn for Helen for eighteen months but it is clear from his introduction to Ghetal's memoir of her mother[187] that he would, as Victoria did for Albert, mourn for her until the day he died: "I cannot be thankful enough to God, that He gave me, for so many years, one who was my friend and counsellor in all things; and who, I knew, was always interceding at a throne of grace for a blessing on me and on my labours."[188]

But in time, though the celibate life may have had much to commend it and the memory of Helen burned deeply in Ridley's heart, the lives of the widowed preacher and the rich spinster from Westbourne Terrace drew closer.

Ridley had two sons who needed a career and a daughter who needed a husband. He had a very busy life and though housekeepers and servants were cheap, the companionship of an intelligent woman, not to mention a substantial income, would be welcome in the autumn of his years.

Esther too, now in her fiftieth year, recognised the benefits of a life with a man who was not only kind and considerate but by now quite famous as a preacher and the writer of several popular and widely translated books. She had no issue of her own to inherit her fortune and she had grown quite fond of the Herschell children over the years.

---

[186] Cholera and typhoid were carried by polluted water; typhus was spread by lice.

[187] *Far above Rubies, Memoirs of H. S. H., by her Daughter,* Edited by R. H. Herschell 1854.

[188] *Ibid*

And so the shrewd Esther, of whom her niece would write, "I think she had more worldly ambition than most of her family," and the wise and often charming Ridley would marry in the summer of 1855.

Although the 1836 *Marriage Act* permitted nonconformist chapels to be registered for marriages the wedding took place at the fashionable St. Marylebone Anglican church, just up the road from Trinity. This was, after all, a society wedding and the Herschell's would not be entering society by the side door on this occasion. The gentrification process would continue when they moved into 124 Gloucester Terrace, Bayswater, close to Esther's attractive property in Westbourne Terrace.

But first, in September 1854, Ridley would make a contribution to the education of his sons that only he could give. Perhaps anticipating the growing role Esther would play in the future of his children he would take the boys, Farrer and Ridley Judah to his and their Fatherland, to the land which in less than a hundred years would once again take the name of Israel.

Ridley Judah already considered himself with some pride to be a Christian Israelite, in modern terms a Messianic Jew. He enjoyed travel and would have welcomed the trip. On the other hand Farrer had always seemed to be more conservative and private in his faith, being described simply as "a strong churchman, and a church-warden at St. Peter's, Eaton Square" in the Jewish Encyclopaedia shortly after his death.

It may be that, like many Jewish people in the mid-19th century, he would choose to withdraw from his Jewish roots. Many years later, as Lord Chancellor of England, he would, according to one obituary, 'buy in'[189] unsold copies of his sister's privately published and printed memoir of their father. As a Liberal MP under the staunchly Anglican Prime Minister Mr Gladstone it would have done him no harm to distance himself from Benjamin Disraeli, Gladstone's overtly Jewish, though baptised, political enemy. And *Burke's Peerage & Baronetage* still endows his father Ridley with the middle name of Henry rather than the Jewish Haim.

---

[189] Unidentified newspaper from Westminster Archives, dated 1899

But for now the scene moves back to what must have been a major adventure for two teenage boys travelling with their father to a distant land. Like all good adventures it started with a sea voyage and the opening lines of Ridley's brief notes on the trip set the scene dramatically: "We left Beirut on Monday, October 2nd, 1854, and directed our course northwards along the sea-coast…"[190]

---

[190] *A Visit To My Fatherland* , Ridley H. Herschell, 1844, Notes of a journey in 1854.

Chapter 34

'There are strings', said Mr Tappertit, '...in the human heart
that had better not be vibrated.'

Charles Dickens, *Barnaby Rudge*

While Farrer and Ridley Judah would get to see all the sights from the Galilee to the Dead Sea and share in the inevitable adventures as they travelled on horseback in a country sadly neglected for two thousand years, Ridley had another more serious agenda.

He had a long cherished plan for a model farm[191] and agricultural school in Palestine, to provide work and future prospects for Jewish Christians in the Land. He developed the idea with local missionaries and shared his vision enthusiastically with the Anglican Bishop of Jerusalem, Michael Solomon Alexander.

On his return to London Ridley presented his ideas to interested parties including Lord Shaftesbury and the Revd. Alfred Augustus Isaacs, a clergyman from Leicester.

Among his many philanthropic interests, from Ragged Schools to the YMCA, Anthony Ashley Cooper, aka Lord Shaftesbury[192], sincerely believed the return of the Jews to Jerusalem would hasten the return of Messiah Jesus, in other words the Second Coming. The population of Jerusalem had grown a hundredfold between 1827 and 1839 largely as a result of the efforts of British Evangelicals like Cooper.

Herschell saw an opportunity to introduce Jewish believers in Jesus into the Land, not necessarily to prepare for the last days but as a means of

---

[191] 18th and 19th century concept of architect-designed farms not necessarily following the local pattern. Notes of a journey in 1854.

[192] 1801-1885

---

relieving the poverty often associated with so-called conversion or apostasy in England. Although Ridley himself would be inclined to leave the future of the world, and the big picture, in the hands of his Creator, he was never averse to furthering his own cause in tandem with others.

Eventually it was Mr Isaacs who took the initiative and bought a *bayara*, a watered plantation, of about ten acres with several buildings from one Manuel Kalis, a resident of Jaffa. Although Herschell played no direct part in the farm's management Mr Isaacs acknowledged his major contribution to the success of the plan, later describing his relationship with him as "a deep and affectionate friendship, which I shall ever regard as one of the most precious of my life." In time the farm flourished and was later run by the London Society for Promoting Christianity amongst the Jews whose descendent, the Church's Ministry among Jewish People (CMJ) is still represented in Jaffa at the Beit Immanuel Congregation and Guest House.

Meanwhile, back on the tour, Ridley and the boys, on their way to the fabled Cedars of Lebanon, are confronted by a farcical scene in a small village:

"Whilst on our way hence to the cedars, we came near a village which seemed all astir; men and women were shrieking, and dogs barking, as though some terrible calamity had befallen them. On hastening to the scene of the uproar, the view that met our eyes was truly ludicrous. On the roof of a house stood a man attempting to pull up a sack by means of a rope, while a priest, aided by some women, was endeavouring to drag the man down; all this was carried on amidst the most hideous noises. At length, the priest getting rather roughly handled, and thinking probably that prudence was the better part of valour, sneaked behind a wall, and kept peeping out to watch the result of the contest. This was soon decided in favour of the man on the roof, the other party being deprived of the valuable assistance of the priest, and the women beginning to beat first their own breasts and then one another."[193]

Ridley seems to have enjoyed these precious weeks with his sons and the joy of their dramatic arrival at Jerusalem must have released him for a time

---

[193] *A Visit To My Fatherland*, Ridley H. Herschell, 1844, Notes of a journey in 1854.

from the pain of bereavement and given him new hope for the future: "Friday, the 20th.October 1854 - Near Abou Goush, about two hours distant from Jerusalem, we were overtaken by a tremendous storm. The effect of the thunder and lightning in the midst of the hills was very grand; but the rain poured down in torrents, and it was no trifling matter riding over slippery rocks with horses already fatigued by twenty days' consecutive. We therefore hailed the sight of Jerusalem, independently of the feelings that always must arise upon viewing that city, with great joy."[194]

Once back in London via a trip down the Nile Ridley was once more constantly occupied, either speaking, travelling or serving his community. The marriage to Esther in 1855 also opened up a new life for him and on their European honeymoon they had dined with the great and the good, and been received by the King and Queen of Prussia. Ridley had arrived. His children would be cared for, they would be financially secure and he was fêted by the rich and famous who sought his advice and listened respectfully to his sermons.

But something was wrong. He seemed to have lost much more than a loving wife and gained so much less than high society could offer him.

Ridley's public prayers probably resembled his private prayers much more than those of a formal liturgy might do. His prayers, like his sermons, always came painfully and simply from the heart and in this petition we have a glimpse of his growing personal struggle with the powers of darkness: "O my God, in the name of the Lord Jesus Christ, my atonement, my friend, my High Priest, I now draw near to Thee. I long to hear Thy voice, and to be guided by Thy counsel; I desire to have my heart enlarged by Thy love. O Lord God, my Father, I place before Thee all my difficulties, trials, and afflictions. Give me to realise that Thy strength is made perfect in my weakness. Whatever thorn in the flesh may trouble me, say Thou unto my soul, 'My grace is sufficient for Thee! O Lord, give me to realise that the Lord Jesus is with me. Nothing that Thou canst give me will satisfy me without Thyself. Deliver me, I beseech

---

[194] Ibid

Thee, from all unbelief; remove all my doubts and fears, and give unto me the assurance of Thy perfect love."

Chapter 35

Methinks I will not die quite happy without having seen
something of that Rome of which I have read so much.
Sir Walter Scott (1771-1832)

March 1857

Two years had passed since the wedding. Ridley was living at what his wife's
relations referred to as "Esther's house." But the work went on at Trinity
Chapel and many travellers passed through Ridley's "home for wayfaring
Jews." Back in the early days at Woolwich he had described his dream as a
place "where the many who gained their livelihood as hawkers could find a
meal, a night's shelter, and a word of Christian kindness. It was hoped that by
this means they might have an opportunity of seeing the effect of Christianity
on the everyday life of its followers, and might thereby be induced to make
themselves acquainted with the religion of Jesus."[195]

The dream had now been fully realised, but the vision was slowly fading.

Esther, recognising that Ridley's health was also suffering, had suggested a
holiday along with her younger sister Caroline. It had been a long cold winter
and they might head south through Europe and even get as far as Rome.
Ridley could call on some of his contacts and mission representatives and
Esther and Caroline could take in the sites and have a good time.

The plan was agreed and early on the Monday morning of 2nd March
1857 Caroline Fuller-Maitland set out from Park Place with her Papa on the
short journey to London, six days before her thirty-seventh birthday and as
excited as a schoolgirl. Her journal of the trip records: Luncheon at Esther's
house, and started with her and Mr. H. by 4 o'clock train to Dover. The Lord
Warden Hotel, talking over our plans in the evening; possibly we may get to

---

[195] *Ibid*

Rome![196]

Mr H. or "the Rabbi" as Caroline would usually call him would, more often than not, leave Esther and her sister to their own devices, with the help, of course, of Jane their shared and ever present maid.

Crossing the Channel they headed down to Paris via Lille more or less following the Grand Tour route through Dijon, Lyon, Avignon, Nimes and the Côte d'Azur, then through the Alps from Genoa to Pisa and Florence.

Arriving in Florence twenty-four days out from London Caroline says, with the rudeness that Herschell by now might have found rather trying, that they had found rooms, "at the Hôtel de New York on the Arno, and went down to the table d'hôte. It was a very crowded one and rather disagreeable. We were too late for the great room and dined in a small one. An Italian woman with a Chinese face sitting at the top, looking fit for any wickedness; the sort of face you would expect Mme. de Brinvilliers or some great criminal to have had. She had a child with her and an English governess. I was very glad I was not the governess."[197]

The next morning Ridley declined the opportunity to visit one of the world's finest museums with the ladies. But Caroline seems to have been as breezy as ever as he parted from them at the entrance of the Uffizi. Her journal records: "Friday, March 27. Our first morning in Florence! The weather bright and delightful. Our windows open at breakfast. Set out afterwards, and went to the post. No letters. Then to the Uffizi Gallery. Mr. H. only just took us in, and left us to wander about in it all the morning."[198]

It was neither the first nor the last time Ridley would be in Florence and the Uffizi and its Renaissance wonders could wait. A more pressing concern was the plight of his Jewish brothers and sisters in the Tuscany capital, though things had improved since his last visit.

---

[196] *How we went to Rome in 1857 by C. F. M.* (Caroline Fuller-Maitland), 1892

[197] *Ibid*

[198] *Ibid*

Until 1848 The Jewish population of Florence had been contained in a ghetto for forty-three years. As in all European countries the Jews of Florence had been treated more or less badly over the centuries according to the whim of the ruling power. The arrangement in Florence had at least been one of mutual tolerance, bearing no resemblance to the later Nazi ghettos of Warsaw or Lodz. But having been released from this medieval apartheid system and given civil rights by Napoleon in 1799 they were especially insulted to be locked up again by the returning and victorious Austrian Hapsburgs in 1814.

While Ridley concerned himself with the spiritual plight of the Jews, and to some extent the ongoing persecution of Protestant Christians, the ladies had found a less serious but historically significant diversion. Nothing less than the invention of the fax machine. Caroline reports: "Monday, March 30. Florence. After breakfast wrote my journal till ½ past 10, when Mr. Stewart called to take us to see the Abate Caselli[199], the inventor of a wonderful improvement in the Electric Telegraph. By his invention writing or drawings can be copied instantaneously at any distance. The Times newspaper may be printed off in America almost at the instant it is printed here. We found Caselli in his studio; he is a thin worn scientific looking man about 40."

Thin and worn as he may have been Signor Caselli would indeed introduce the first commercial facsimile (fax) system between Lyon and Paris in 1863. The world was changing very rapidly.

And so, taking the 5 o'clock train to Sienna, the little group set off for Rome, down through the green heart of Italy, arriving in the future Capital for Palm Sunday, 1857. Caroline sets the scene with her usual indiscretion: "The Pope is busy at 8 o'clock giving away palms in St. Peter's", she records, "but we did not go to see him."

This undiplomatic snub to Pius IX was somewhat ameliorated by Caroline buying a palm allegedly blessed by His Holiness while out for a walk on the Corso with Jane. They went instead to the service in the chapel of the American Legation. Avoiding the proceedings at St. Peter's was perhaps

---

[199] Giovanni Caselli (1815-1891)

understandable for, even under this reforming Pope, Protestant worship was still only allowed to visiting forcigners. There were still no alternatives to Roman Catholicism for most people although ironically the Jews were now free to practice their faith anywhere in Rome. Pope Pius IX had finally closed the ghetto in 1848.

Again on Easter Sunday they worshiped at the American chapel where Ridley was invited to preach. Summing up the rest of the day Caroline confides to her journal: "We dined in our own room. The Rabbi Consola and another Jew called to have some talk with Mr. Herschell and Esther and I walked out to the Corso Gardens and Pincian Hill. I was at home in the evening, Esther and Mr. H. having tea at Mrs. Coventry's. There was no illumination of St. Peter's; it was said to have been put off in expectation of the coming of the Russian Empress, but as her coming was really not expected, the real reason must be either want of money or fear of insurrection. I was not sorry, for I did not mean to go to see it, and yet should have been vexed at missing it, the great sight of the Easter Week in Rome."[200]

Mr Herschell dutifully toured the city with his wife and sister-in-law, but the strain of sightseeing seems to have been all too much for Caroline and even the glorious Sistine Chapel could not, in the end, keep her from her tea: "The roof is entirely by Michael Angelo, and the great fresco of the Last judgment is also his. We were too tired when we came away from the sculpture to attempt to take in this wonderful Sistine chapel. Its richness of colour was almost all I could see, for I was quite tired out with looking, and straining my little mind after the sculptures. So we came to a shop and had some buns, and then went to buy some photographs. Afterwards Esther and I walked to a shop, and then with Mr. H. to the gardens of the Corso. After the table d'hôte I wrote to Mamma, and went to bed."[201]

31st April 1857. The long journey to the sun was drawing to a close. Under the smoke blackened girders of the old north station in Paris, still chilly

---

[200] *How we went to Rome in 1857 by C. F. M.* (Caroline Fuller-Maitland), 1892

[201] *Ibid*

in the early spring sunshine, Ridley was feeling the burdens of his fiftieth year. He was no longer a young man and Paris had few attractions for him now. Soon the old building would be replaced, like so much in this middle-aged century of progress, and would become the present day Gare du Nord. The old station would be transported north where it remains to this day as Lille-Flanders. Perhaps Ridley himself was to be replaced like the old railway terminus, he thought. Perhaps his mission had finished, terminated by a demanding God, or perhaps he had failed in his ministry or just lost his way. Perhaps God never had given him that work to do in the first place and, the question entered his mind slyly and imperceptibly, had the Messiah of Israel really spoken to him in this wretched city so many years ago?

Black smoke and steam suddenly choked his murmured doubts and prayers. Red and orange coals of fire seemed to burn his face and the iron rails screamed under the weight of their creaking burden as the steam engine pulled slowly and heavily out, into the heartless northern suburbs of the Faubourg Saint Denis. Ridley slept.

After some time the countryside began to open up before the speeding train and the warm morning sun flickered through the windows of the first class carriage. Soon they would be in London and work would overtake him again. God could rebuild him while the old vision still flickered in his aching heart. His own words of advice to another, partly quoting Homer, came quietly back as if to rebuke him, urging him to hold fast: "Be swift as a stag and strong as a lion to do the will of thy heavenly Father."[202]

Caroline glanced at the Rabbi and he smiled at her. She seemed to have few enough doubts and fears about her own life or her small privileged world. She smiled back without really knowing why and returned to her book. Like so many before her and so many more to come, all she really wanted now was a proper cup of tea: "Thursday, April 31. Paris to Folkestone. At the railway station before we left Paris I saw a round red balloon in a shop close by; I could not walk quite so far, my back being weak, but I sent Jane the maid with

[202] Anonymous letter

my purse and she bought the red balloon for 2 francs. It was full of gas, and ready to go up into infinite space, if it were not held down by a string. I kept it in my hand all the way to Boulogne. There we went on board the steamboat, and for two hours I was obliged to lie down in the cabin and I forgot my red balloon. When we got to the Pavilion Hotel at Folkestone I asked a man to get it for me from the custom house where it had been taken from the steamboat cabin. He said a lady had been there, and had claimed it and taken it away; I greatly hoped that the "lady" was Jane the maid, who had been sent off to London with our luggage. So here we were on our own old English ground again. I put my head out of the window and liked the smell of the grass; it was so different to the bright dry air of Italy. Then Esther and I had a real English tea, a very great one, in a plain square English room. I was very heartily glad to see the old things again. Esther and the Rabbi walked out in the evening; I could not walk but went to bed about 8."[203]

---

[203] *How we went to Rome in 1857 by C. F. M.* (Caroline Fuller-Maitland), 1892

Chapter 36

Do good by stealth, and blush to find it fame.

Alexander Pope (1688-1744)

Back in London Ridley had become a celebrity, and like most celebrities, whether in entertainment, politics or evangelism, his life had to some extent been taken over by his own team of helpers. He would have an appointment with Lord or Lady so and so, a visit to, or from, an important representative of this or that organisation, not to mention his own missionaries in the field who needed to see him from time to time. When he spoke, people listened. When he wrote people bought his books by the thousands. Many of the eight volumes he had written by 1857 had been translated into French, German and Dutch.

He would also be expected to preach at most of the morning services, but his brother David was now playing a major part in the day to day running of Trinity chapel, relieving Ridley for the more high profile work. The Revd. David Abraham Herschell[204] would even lead many of the morning services now.

A hundred years later Ridley's relaxed but authoritative style would have made him a popular television pundit, as this 1857 "sound bite" from the third Evangelical Alliance conference in Berlin shows:

"I believe there is nothing that we Christian Israelites ought more earnestly to seek to maintain than our distinct nationality. We must show our brethren that in becoming Christians we have not ceased to be Jews. Our national life and expectations are based upon the word and promise of God, and can never be abandoned."

This profoundly simple summary of the modern Messianic Jewish

---

[204] David Abraham Herschell (1823-1904)

movement would have shocked much of the Church and society. This was no "convert" from Judaism speaking. This man had not been baptised in order to make his way in a so-called Christian country, like the future Prime Minister Benjamin Disraeli had been. Neither was he an assimilated immigrant falling in with the local customs and religion. They were in the presence of a missing link, a throwback to the Church in Jerusalem, and the Jewish Church in Rome to whom St. Paul had written his Epistle.

Herschell represented a line of Messianic faith directly from Jerusalem, even bypassing the very name of Christian first used in Antioch in the time of Paul and Barnabas[205] and now hated by most Jews for its associations with persecution.

This man was a follower of *Yeshua Ha Mashiach*, Jesus the Messiah, the Christ who worshipped on the Jewish Sabbath, Shabbat (Luke 4:16), celebrated the Jewish holidays of Passover and Chanukah (Matthew 26:17, John 10:22) and even wore the traditional tzitzit or fringed shawl (Matthew 9:20). He worshipped the Anointed One whose mother was the Jewess Miriam (Mary) and whose earthly father would have given him the common Jewish name of Yeshua Ben Joseph.

This Messianic faith, which paralleled and complimented the traditional Church's teaching, where it conformed with Scripture, was set to become either a new third way, yet another denomination, or an opportunity for healing in the Body of Christ. The "separated brethren" of the Roman Catholic Church[206], along with her Orthodox sister, and the breakaway Protestants had for many centuries almost completely lost track of their Jewish roots. Even by the time of the Council of Nicea in 325 none of the 318 bishops who attended had Jewish origins and for the later Protestants the advice of Martin Luther in dealing with the Jews was:

"First to set fire to their synagogues or schools and to bury and cover with dirt whatever will not burn, so that no man will ever again see a stone or

---

[205] Acts 11:26

[206] *Vatican II*, Decree on Ecumenism

cinder of them. This is to be done in honour of our Lord and of Christendom, so that God might see that we are Christians, and do not condone or knowingly tolerate such public lying, cursing, and blaspheming of his Son and of his Christians."[207]

Somewhere down the line the teaching of St. Paul had been lost. To say that the roots of the Christian Church were firmly planted in the Jewish faith is much more than just a recognition of Abraham and Moses as token members of the family. Many faiths, particularly Islam, acknowledge the Jewish faith as a foundation of their beliefs. But for Gentile Christians the connection to the root was not made by taking a cutting or simply by planting similar seeds. St. Paul compares it to grafting a wild olive tree onto the original plant so that only God, the creator, could ever separate it.[208]

Since the creation of the State of Israel in 1948 there has been a new awareness among Christians and many others, of the Jewish people as a nation. But for centuries they had been seen as a wandering band of introverted misfits. To many they had been the "Christ-killers", to others they had been the rejected chosen people of an angry God. To the demonic creators of the Holocaust they were less than nothing, and the Church, for the most part, averted its eyes.

How was it possible that Gentile Christians could presume now to look for unity through the Jews in a Church that had persecuted, denied and ignored them for so long? They didn't have to. Slowly, and in God's good time, through people like Ridley Herschell, they were reaching out to the Church, with forgiveness.

While he was in Berlin Ridley took the opportunity to speak to the many visiting Messianic Jews about the farm in Jaffa. A large number of inquisitive unconverted Jews also attended and filled the galleries of the Church of the Holy Ghost which he had hired for the occasion. He spoke to them too and Ghetal tells us he was listened to with: "the most marked and respectful atten-

---

[207] *The Jews And Their Lies*, Martin Luther, 1543

[208] Romans 11:17-21

tion. He dwelt much on one of his favourite themes, the love of the Christian Israelite for his people and country, assuring those whom he addressed that this were always intensified by genuine love to Christ. The effect of this address was seen on the following Saturday when he went to the synagogue. As soon as he was observed, two of the congregation went to him and escorted him to the seat of honour between the two principal rabbis. He was treated with the utmost respect, and afterwards had the opportunity of some profitable conversation with a few of their number."

But Herschell the celebrity was only going through the motions. He knew his lines, he knew the story. He had all the answers. But just three years before, on the first anniversary of Helen's death he had confided: "She has been so vividly before me for the last few days, that I have felt more keenly her loss than I have yet done." And in a moment of agonizing honesty he writes: "Alas! I feel very low, and am tempted to fear that I am a lost sinner; I feel very weak in soul and mind, a kind of sensation as if God had utterly forsaken me. I still do trust in Him, and the full salvation I have preached for so many years is my plea before God - 'Jesus Christ, the same yesterday, today, and for ever.'"

Three years on he was exhausted. He had worked himself into the ground, but more in his own strength than in faith. Esther had found her own innate strength and the faith to stay by his side, but she too by now was in need of rest. She insisted they spend some time together in the Isle of Wight, a few miles off the south coast of England. Just an hour or so by paddle steamer across the Solent from Portsmouth but somehow isolated from the frantic life of the mainland, as Queen Victoria found when she escaped regularly to her own island home of Osborne House.

But even here, in the quiet seaside town of Ryde, his fame had spread and Ridley was called on to work:

He was urgently requested to take part in outdoor services in the poorest part of the town. For this purpose a tent was erected, open at the sides, and so placed that the people in the neighbouring cottages could, if they chose, listen from their doors or windows. Here, on several Sunday afternoons, he gave those homely, simple, heart-stirring addresses, which he well knew how to adapt to the condition of his audience. In spite of the unexpected work the periods of rest had brought Herschell back from the brink of collapse, but Esther determined that after the next few month's commitments, including the major trip to Germany, she would get him away from the crowds and the constant pressure. They would tour Wales, meeting a few friends, keeping on the move and visiting castles. Perhaps she thought the religiously conservative Welsh would not be attracted by the novelty of a Jewish Nonconformist preacher. Or perhaps she just hoped a country the size of modern Israel with the population of Paris, just over a million at the time, might be the place to get lost for a while. Whatever her thinking, in the summer of 1858 they set off for the Welsh border, leaving brother David in charge.

At Tenby, its rocky promontory overlooking the white sandy beaches of Carmarthen Bay, God appears to have caught up with Ridley Herschell and, like his father Jacob at the ford of the Jabbok, Ridley would receive a blessing and an affliction after his long struggle.[209]

---

[209] Genesis 32:22-32

Chapter 37

Tempora mutantur, et nos mutamur in illis
(Times change, and we change with them)
Christoph Cellarius (1638 - 1707)

Tenby was to be their last port of call in the Principality. Esther had stuck to her plan that they should visit castles and Carew was the last on her list. It was 1st September 1858 and they were due back in London in two days. Ridley would later confess that during the whole journey he had been, "secretly mourning over the coldness and deadness of his heart in spiritual things, and that he felt a great unwillingness to return to his ministerial labours."

As they were walking away from the castle Ridley seemed preoccupied and was some distance from the rest of them. He appeared to slip and fall. He would not have appreciated any help in getting up so they waited for him to regain his feet, and his dignity. But he didn't get up. Instead he cried out, "Thank God, I have broken my leg; thank God for it!" The party were stunned. Then Esther lifted her skirts and set off across the stony ground.

"It's all right, I'm very happy," were the first words he spoke to her as she rushed up to him, breathless and flushed with the unaccustomed exertion. He must have been in agonising pain, but he added quietly, "This is God's answer to my prayer." Some relief for the pain may have been offered in the form of laudanum but Ridley knew the addictive properties of the popular opium and alcohol based drug and he probably would not have taken it. Relief was to come in rather more unexpected ways. First he was taken to a nearby cottage where the occupier had once experienced a broken leg himself. Then, at the same time as they arrived, the assistant-surgeon of a Royal Navy ship, a man-of-war, coming with a party from Pembroke Dock to visit the ruins also appeared. The occupier of the cottage provided bandages and splints and the surgeon set the bone. It wasn't for nothing that ship's surgeons were known as sawbones. Much of their work involved either fast amputations or fixing broken bones. Ridley could not have asked for a better person to arrive at that moment.

Once the leg had been skilfully set arrangements were made for the seven mile journey to Tenby. A cart with a feather mattress and pillows was offered and they set out for their lodgings.

During the painful and often sleepless weeks that followed Ridley clearly believed, as he did at the time it happened, that he had encountered the living God in time and space and been struck down: "This day three weeks the Lord visited me. I look back to it with feelings of solemn and intense interest; and although the three weeks seem very long, I remember every day with thankfulness."

He doesn't seem to have acknowledged the providential arrival of the assistant-surgeon as part of God's plan to lessen his suffering but talks much of his "earnest wrestling prayer" and writes to his church about the dramatic response to his decline since the death of Helen:

"I cannot look at it in any other light, because I had cried to God, and humbled myself before Him on account of my low state, and had asked Him not to permit me to go back to my labours amongst you until my faith should be revived, and my heart fuller of the love of Christ. In answer to my solemn prayers for my soul and yours, the Lord touched me as clearly as He did Jacob. I fell down as I was standing still, and found myself lying with my broken leg resting on the other. When I saw this I was filled at once with praise and thanksgiving to God for His mercy and love to me."

Ridley had been pulled back from the brink of a burnout, a breakdown. He would not be back at Trinity Chapel for six months, and they would get by without him. God seems to have wanted him out of action, disabled for a while, to prepare him for what was to come. Ghetal, perceptive and sensitive as ever, writes from her home in Oxford:

"Many weary days and nights of pain were his portion before he was again able to resume his work; but many lessons of trust and love and patience were learned by him during his time of seclusion. Though the suffering was often intense, and the long sleepless nights were especially trying, yet he was full of

178

peace, and was able to rejoice in the Lord, and to thank Him for the affliction which had brought such happiness to his soul."

They remained in Tenby for three months, until the end of November 1858 when an invalid carriage was sent from London to take him home. The journey would take three days but he would not resume his duties until late in the spring of 1859.

In many ways the restless Victorian world had moved on and Ridley would need to reassess his life and his work in the light of God's new direction for him. In 1858 Lionel de Rothschild had become the first Jewish MP to be permitted to take his seat without taking the oath that involved the words "by the true faith of a Christian". Ridley's own eldest son, having taken his BA at London University, entered the chambers of lawyer Thomas Chitty[210] in 1858, eventually becoming a barrister and an MP himself.

A Jewish welfare organization for the poor called the Board of Guardians for the Relief of the Jewish Poor, today Jewish Care, was created in 1859. And Mr Charles Darwin published his *Origin of Species* introducing the theory of evolution to a world hungry for new ideas. And the world, if not the species, was evolving fast.

The philanthropic relief to be found in the Herschell's "home for wayfaring Jews" was giving way to the beginnings of community care. By 1861 the home at 37 Newnham Street was described in the national census as "unoccupied". Ridley and Helen's old house at 36 Newnham Street, next to the chapel, had two families in it, an elderly lady called Elizabeth Burrows with her two daughters and a Mr Jacob Mayer from Germany and his household, described as a "Missionary to the Jews".

Ridley too would now concentrate his work in the community, his community, whether Jewish or gentile, rich or poor. And his travelling too would be curtailed as a result of his broken leg and the poor health which he was feeling more and more. Sometimes he would even be pushed in a Bath chair to get around more easily and the nearby Victoria Station meant his

---

[210] 1802-1878

travels would often be restricted to the fashionable south coast resort of Brighton.

But there was another seaside resort, closer to his heart than Brighton, and, by one of those chance encounters he so often seems to have had, Ridley found himself drawn back to the fishing village at Leigh-on-Sea:

"Going out one day in his Bath chair," writes Esther, "he met an old acquaintance from the neighbourhood of Leigh - the tenant of a large farm of Lady Olivia Sparrow - who at once recognised him, although after an interval of twenty-four years."

The news that the man had to tell of the progress made and the fruits of the Herschells' labours was so exciting that Ridley, in spite of a still demanding schedule of preaching and teaching, determined to go there to see for himself.

Travelling down on the new London, Tilbury and Southend Railway, in the summer of 1859, they checked in to the once fashionable Royal Hotel in Southend, designated royal following visits by Princess Caroline, wife of the Prince Regent in 1803.

The next day they drove over to Leigh and down Leigh Hill to the old fishing village, now peaceful and busy under a cloudless summer sky. Ridley looked up to the dominating church of St. Clement, patron saint of boatmen, mariners and sailors, breathing deeply on the intoxicating mix of sea, black mud and shellfish that permeated the cobbled streets and alleys below them. Up there, close to the church, was the old school and the cottage he had shared with Helen and the two girls, Ghetal and baby Esther. He could quite happily live here, a fisher of men among the fishermen of old Leigh. It was so hard to believe the changes that had taken place in twenty-four years. Esther had never seen him so happy and left him to his memories as they clattered slowly past the cottages and shops of Leigh Road. Then it happened, from somewhere across the street, a gruff voice calling out, Esther jumped. Ridley turned round in his seat and stopped the carriage. It was a moment of recognition from half a lifetime ago. "Mr Herschell!" Three old fishermen had recognised their friend and benefactor.

Soon the whole village knew he was there. Windows were flung open and children brought half dressed out to the front step. It was as if John Wesley himself had ridden into town, as indeed he had many years before. But who was this man, asked the younger generation. And who was the lady, asked the older. They would all know soon enough.

Chapter 38

Poverty and oysters always seem to go together.

Charles Dickens, *The Pickwick Papers*

Further down the Leigh Road between the hills and the marshes lived the fishermen. Over 200 men and boys were engaged in fishing for shrimps in Leigh. Up to two thousand gallons of the small translucent crustacean could be sent to London and a hundred gallons might be caught by just one shrimp boat crew in a day. Shrimps had long overtaken oysters and whelks as the local industry, and the fisherman's life was still hard and dangerous.

At number thirteen lived a fisherman Ridley particularly longed to see again. Ever since the evening nearly twenty-five years ago when he had walked out of Herschell's meeting convinced and convicted that he was a sinner in need of the Messiah's love Michael Tomlin had been sharing and preaching the good news of Jesus. Perhaps God had brought Ridley back to Leigh to show him the fruit of his early labours in the vineyard. Whatever had brought them to Leigh the Herschells had arranged to call on Michael and his family before they returned to London.

They arrived at the cottage with flowers for Mrs Tomlin and some small presents for their many children. The two men were so different thought Esther as she prepared to leave them alone to talk. The small educated Jew, frock coated, watch chain, waistcoat and shining leather shoes, and the giant Michael, his great sea of a beard rising and falling in the light breeze as he closed the cottage door with hands like barnacled rocks and introduced them to his wife Elizabeth.

Ridley already knew Michael had faced many attacks on his faith in the early days. How he had been in charge of an oyster dredger and was required to work on a Sunday. "Betty," he had said, "I cannot go out on a Sunday, even if we starve."[211]

Ridley already knew how the owner had taken the vessel and his livelihood away from him leaving them to live on charity or the parish. And he already knew he had taken casual work unloading oysters to make a few shillings and how he had prayed that "God would make a way of escape for him."[212]

And, above all, he already knew how that prayer had been answered when, a few hours later, there was a knock on the cottage door. It was the owner of Michael's boat. He said: "I cannot rest since I stopped you going out in my boat, I have had no peace of mind. You can take the vessel out and not go out on Sundays; if you want any money I will lend you some."[213]

Soon after that time of testing for Michael, Ridley had left for Brampton at the request of Lady Sparrow to face his own challenges and had lost touch with Michael and Betty, neither of whom could read or write. So there was much to catch up on though Michael had heard about the death of Helen. They spoke briefly and arranged to meet again soon, but not before Ridley had discovered something of the extent of Michael's part time ministry as a full time fisherman. How he had joined the first Methodist chapel in Leigh and been mysteriously invited to speak at another chapel, thirty miles away, when the preacher found himself unable to preach. How he had been encouraged to learn to read and write (his favourite books, apart from the Bible, became Bunyan's *Pilgrim's Progress* and *Grace Abounding*).

Michael had even preached in the open air from an old barge on the beach at Southend, often being mocked and shouted down by the crowd that gathered. Later a room was found for him to preach in and it became known, not surprisingly as the Upper Room. Many years later a merchant from Billingsgate fish market told Michael's son Stephen:

"When I was a lad I went to the upper room and came down with my heart changed and no one ever went up to that room and came down the

---

[211] *Michael Tomlin, A Fisher of Men*, S.F. Johnson, 1945.

[212] *Ibid*

[213] *Ibid*

same."[214]

Ridley asked if Michael had ever considered going into the ministry full-time. Yes, he said, as it happened a number of people were considering that possibility even now. Recently a very successful Mission had been held led by Michael and, according to one of his supporters, James Guiver, it was, "very successful and there was a great revival and many decided for Christ, and the work went on so well and so fast that the leading friends and supporters of the work began to think of having a larger place. So they decided to build a new Chapel and have Mr Tomlin for their minister."[215]

Mr Tomlin himself had not yet agreed to this proposal and what transpired between him and Ridley on the subject has not been recorded. But by their next meeting Michael had made his decision. Stephen Johnson records in his 1945 biography[216] of Michael Tomlin:

"…the call did come very definitely, for one day when he had pulled the last net on board, he said to his mate, "There they are, they will never go over the side again by me." From that day he left his nets and his boat 'Betty' to become a full-time 'fisher of men.' His choice was to be richly blessed, for he had shown by his service that he was worthy to follow in the footsteps of the Galilean fishermen who, left their nets to follow Him who still calls to-day."

Ridley and Esther had planned to return to Leigh in a couple of weeks to hold a party for all Ridley's old friends and their children, just like the one for Lady Olivia when she had visited the school. The two unlikely evangelists, Michael Tomlin and Ridley Herschell, parted as friends, divided in many ways by the world, but united for ever in their faith. They would meet again soon. As they left Michael mentioned to Mr Herschell, he would always call him Mr Herschell, that Ivy Cottage, Ridley's old home on Leigh Hill, was up for sale. Ridley smiled thoughtfully and gently took the arm of his very rich wife. They would talk about it on the way back to London.

---

[214] *Ibid*

[215] *Ibid*

[216] *Ibid*

Two weeks later, after the tent party for two hundred and fifty people and the open-air meeting which followed for the crowds that gathered outside, Ridley and his party went to view the cottage. In the summer of 1860 it was ready for occupation and the Herschells took possession.[217] A Chapel School had been built by Ridley at the bottom of the long garden to replace Lady Sparrow's old school, sold in the wind up of her affairs shortly before her death. Like the old school, the new chapel school would be known as Herschell's School.

In 1847 Robert Eden, Rector of St. Clement's and a wealthy man, had founded a National School in Leigh under the Church of England's authority following conflicts with Lady Olivia and her unorthodox views. Ridley would ensure the nonconformist tradition would carry on for many years and Michael Tomlin would preach there regularly until his own chapel was ready.

By Spring the following year a site had been secured for Tomlin's new chapel and a Trust Deed gave power to "raise money by way of mortgage" for its construction. The Free Methodist Chapel was opened on the 13th October 1861 and on Sunday, August 10th 1862 the Revd. Ridley Herschell preached at the morning service to celebrate the first anniversary of its founding. The Rabbi and the fisherman, the scholar and the labourer, were working together in the Master's vineyard.

---

[217] Then known as Ivy Cottage, it is today called Herschell House

Chapter 39

Constitutional liberty will be best worked out by those
who aspire to freedom by their own efforts.
Sir Robert Peel (1788-1850)

Herschell's influence was international and far reaching. Fêted by the rich and famous, loved by his humble parishioners, his simple gospel message influenced generations. He was among the founders of the Evangelical Alliance[218], Christian Witness to Israel[219] and many other organisations worldwide. He travelled widely and had spoken to thousands of people from Europe to Israel and beyond. He accepted poverty and material comfort with equanimity and trust, knowing that neither was permanent. But by the 1860s his ministry at home had become the centre of his life.

He continued to write and in 1860 published his last book, *Strength in Weakness, A Meditation on Some of the Psalms*, reflecting his own condition as he responded to the burden of physical weakness.

In spite of poor health he planned a trip to Italy and was a regular visitor to Brighton and his cottage in Leigh. But Marylebone was his parish and the tired evangelist, like his friend Michael Tomlin, was now a pastor. He offered his gifts to the local people, Jew and gentile, and they responded, like the Psalmist's deer, and drank from the stream he offered them in the Gospel.[220]

"In 1860," writes Ghetal, "my father's thoughts were first specially directed to the religious condition of the police force, one of whom was a member of his congregation."

The spiritual needs of the police had, it seems, been sadly neglected.

---

[218] Evangelical Alliance: www.eauk.org

[219] Christian Witness to Israel: www.cwi.org.uk

[220] Psalm 42:1

Sailors, soldiers, navvies, and cabmen all had their special missionaries but Robert Peel's Police force, only extended beyond London to the provinces in 1856, had not always been popular. People of all classes had seen them as infringing their personal liberty in one way or another.

Ridley would take them under his wing, or at least the police of D Division in Marylebone. And so, on 5th April 1860 the first of a series of Friday afternoon meetings was held. Twelve policemen turned up, in their own time, to take tea with Ridley and to read and discuss the Scriptures. Soon after the first meeting fifty or sixty were attending, and the tea was dropped, at the request of the men, in order to concentrate on the teaching.

Ridley had the rare gift, like Paul of Tarsus, of almost effortlessly being "all things all men."

"To the weak I became weak, to win the weak. I have become all things to all men so that by all possible means I might save some."[221]

As one of the constables put it, "He understood us so well, he was just like one of us. We used to say, he only wanted the uniform!"

---

[221] 1 Corinthians 9:22

Chapter 40

"Let China sleep, for when she wakes the world will tremble,"
Napoleon Bonaparte (1769-1821)

By the time the youngest Herschell, Ridley Judah, arrived in Shanghai in 1862 the Opium Wars were over and the Chinese subdued.

Since 1800 British merchants, with the support of the British government and later the French, had been freely supplying opium from India to the Chinese people on a massive commercial scale. Two efforts by the Chinese to stop the fatal supply resulted in devastating wars with the British. The first from 1839 to 1843, the second, and decisive, from 1856 to 1860. The end result was the humiliation of China in the face of overwhelming military power and the ceding of Hong Kong, Shanghai and many other ports to the British and their European and American allies. The occupation of Beijing and the legalisation of the opium trade in China were among many other indignities imposed on the defeated nation. In 1800 there were an estimated two million opium addicts in China. Long before the end of the century a conservative estimate was 30 to 40 million.

That Ridley should allow his son to play a small part in this most un-Christian occupation of another country is for others to judge. One thing was clear, the British and their friends were there to stay, and they stayed for a hundred years or more, only finally leaving Hong Kong in 1997.

Shanghai had become one of the busiest ports in the world, living up to its romantic image of intrigue, shady dealings and exotic night life. The Bund with its grand colonial buildings stretching along the edge of the Huangpu river would be developed into the showpiece of a teeming metropolis which would become known in time as the "Paris of the East". Opportunities abounded for young middle class British men and the twenty-two year old Ridley Judah would seek his fortune, or at least a business education, here on this eastern frontier of the British Empire.

Elder brother Farrer had been called to the bar in 1860 and had himself considered going to Shanghai to practice law in the consular courts. Ghetal had settled down in Oxford with her physician husband John, one day to be Sir John Scott Burdon-Sanderson, and Mary had married into the Cunliffe banking family[222] who naturally had connections with the Shanghai and Hong Kong banks. It was hard to avoid.

If, on his return to London, Ridley could see his youngest son settled in business, which he seemed too have an aptitude for, he would consider his worldly duty done to his children.

But Ridley Judah would never return to England. Within a few weeks of arriving in Shanghai his old coughing fits returned. They had hoped his long stay in southern Europe would have been beneficial, and indeed it was. While in Nice in the South of France his health so much improved that he wrote home with his usual light humour, "I think I have forgotten how to cough."

In December 1859 he wrote enthusiastically, in his small closely joined handwriting, of the places and people he had got to know. But he looked forward to returning home.

"I can hardly think of a single place I have been to, where I have not met somebody who has called and invited me to his house. I find now that I must pull up quite short, or I shall be getting beyond the set amongst whom alone I want to move."

A sensitive and loving son, Ghetal calls him the "apple of the eye" to his parents, he would probably have enjoyed a quieter more private life than the one he inherited. His letters to his sister Mary seem introspective and full of sighs. "O Mary," he writes as he pours out his heart. Mary had visited him in France and he seems to have treasured that time with her.

When he finally leaves obediently for Shanghai, after working two years for a merchant in London, Ridley Judah again corresponds affectionately with his sister. From somewhere at sea, a week out of Southampton he writes:

---

[222] John Cunliffe, uncle of Walter Cunliffe, a future governor of the Bank of England (1913)

"My dearest Mary,

How are you? I hope you didn't catch cold on that black Thursday . . . What a day that was! The rain, and dullness, and cold - and associations will always be present to my mind. We are a queer set of beings though, - and it is a great blessing that we adapt ourselves so easily to a change of circumstances. Just think that a week ago I parted, for the first time, from all that I loved and cared for in the world; and that here I am to-day on the open sea, feeling as jolly and happy as possible."

Ridley Judah would write home every two weeks from China, never missing the mail boat. Then one day the letter didn't come. Three months. Six letters. And now, in the middle of June, nothing. A dreadful, foreboding silence.

Of course there might be a hundred reasons for the delay. Ridley Judah may have been busy and disastrously missed the post. He might have been unwell at the time, who knows what ailments could overtake you in that far off land and, being bedridden for a while perhaps, forgot to give his letter to a friend to take to the post office.

When the mail did arrive from Shanghai, two weeks later, Ridley recognised the cold, empty void that came over him when he had received that awful note from Bonn. He knew this too was not good news. It was not from his son. It was from the British Consulate and formally announced that on 27th July 1862 Ridley Judah Herschell, at the age of twenty-two, had died in Shanghai, China. He had been buried in the new cemetery at the London Mission Compound on Shantung Road.

Chapter 41

Hold thou thy cross before my closing eyes.

Hymn, *Abide With Me*, Henry F. Lyte, (1793-1847)

Although the healing properties of the mud at Southend and Leigh were probably more real than those of the sea water at Brighton it was still much more acceptable in society to "take the waters" at the more fashionable Sussex spa than to "take the mud" at Southend-on-Sea. And so it probably was that Ridley found himself more often in Brighton with Esther than in his beloved Leigh as his health declined. But all the waters and all the mud in the world could not heal Ridley's broken heart. They walked along the front together day after day, Ridley and Esther. Sometimes a nurse would push him in his Bath chair. Always together. He had grown fond of her, and she loved him in her way, and cared for him to the end.

There were times when he rallied and made plans. He even made a trip to Italy, not only for his health, but to see Jewish friends in Naples and missionaries around the country. He longed to see the new mission station which he had set up in what the British called Leghorn on the Ligurian Sea. To Italians it was the port of Livorno, emigration and departure point for New York and arrival point for those tourists who could not face the overland journey to Tuscany.

He took the opportunity to visit Pompeii, the city destroyed with two thousand souls when Mount Vesuvius erupted in AD 79. Ghetal recalls: "My father was greatly impressed with Pompeii, and alluded more frequently to his visit to it than to any other portion of his journey. He said he could preach several discourses on the thoughts suggested by that ruined city."

On his homeward journey, Ridley was taken ill and was confined to bed for two days. As soon as he could get up, he determined to travel home as quickly as his strength would allow, and arrived in London on the 16th of December 1863.

By March the following year his health had deteriorated to the point where he could not receive the many visitors who wanted to call on him. He could have gone to the cottage in Leigh but there too he was well known, and much loved. So they would go to Brighton, where, for want of any more real medical help, says Mrs Herschell optimistically, "the sea-breezes might exert a beneficial influence upon his health."

There, at 105 King's Road, he would sit at his window and watch the timeless tide climb up the hard beach, only to fall back, losing its watery grip on the smooth stones. Like Ridley, it could not hold on to what was not its own. God had given and was now taking away. His favourite Psalm, the 23rd, accompanied his thoughts like an old companion…

יְהֹוָה רֹעִי לֹא אֶחְסָר

"The Lord is my shepherd," said the English translation he had known for so long, "I shall not want."

"Before I knew the Lord He kept me from falling. What dangers He has preserved me from - precipices on the brink of which I stood ready to plunge down - but He prevented me. I should have made shipwreck over and over again if He had not saved me - in Irving's time, and at other periods."

He maketh me to lie down in green pastures…

"He held me, I did not do it myself. Goodness and mercy! You can't set yourself to believe this - to reflect upon it as a task - you must realise it as you look back upon your life."[223]

He leadeth me beside the still waters…

"If ever I preach again I will tell the people more of the love of God. It is not the doctrine of election or any other doctrine - as a doctrine - that gives me comfort now; but to know that God is my Father. I rest simply on the love of God; that is all my religion now."

He restoreth my soul…

---

[223] Incidents in the Life of Ridley Herschell, *Memories of Gospel Triumphs Among the Jews During the Victorian Era*, John Dunlop, 1894

"To know that God is my Father, and Jesus Christ my Saviour, this is my comfort now."

He leadeth me in the paths of righteousness for his name's sake…

Yea, though I walk through the valley of the shadow of death,

I will fear no evil: for thou art with me;

thy rod and thy staff they comfort me.

Thou preparest a table before me in the presence of mine enemies:

thou anointest my head with oil; my cup runneth over.

Surely goodness and mercy shall follow me all the days of my life:

and I will dwell in the house of the Lord for ever.

Ridley Haim Herschell died of heart and renal failure in Brighton on Thursday 14th April 1864. His family were present, including two of his ordained brothers, David and Louis. Victor was a curate in Jamaica and Ridley was spared the news of his brutal murder in 1865.

On 20th April three hundred policemen of D Division, all that could be spared, followed the funeral cortège from Trinity Chapel to Kensal Green Cemetery. Hundreds more from among the great and the good and his local congregation attended the funeral to pay their last respects to a man who had touched all their lives at some point.

A large stone monument, supported by eight pillars and bearing the name HERSCHELL in bold capital letters, was later erected and still stands today, close to the entrance of the cemetery. The inscription on it reads:

"In memory of Reverend Ridley H. Herschell late Minister of Trinity Chapel, John Street, Edgware. A Hebrew by birth - educated in the Jewish faith, converted in early youth to belief in Christ and evermore devoted to the service of his Master. Honoured labourer in the dissemination of Christian truth at home and abroad. An enlightened expounder of the Old and New Testament Scriptures. A fearless monitor and sympathising friend this monument is erected over his remains by his friends and members of his congregation aided by a contribution from the D division of the Metropolitan Police in whose welfare he took a special interest as a record of their affection, esteem, and gratitude, and a token of their grief. He departed this life 14th day of April 1864 aged 57."

In 1882 Esther died in Brighton and was interred under the same monument.

Helen's grave lies sadly neglected, its headstone broken in two and the words obscured beyond recognition, close to the canal at the back of the cemetery. Perhaps it read, we may never know, "Who can find a virtuous woman? for her price is far above rubies."

THE END

Bibliography

Published Works of Ridley Haim Herschell

1834, A BRIEF SKETCH OF THE PRESENT STATE AND FUTURE EXPECTATIONS OF THE JEWS: IN A LETTER ADDRESSED TO HIS CHRISTIAN FRIENDS, BY R.H.H.

1842, REASONS WHY I, A JEW, HAVE BECOME A CATHOLIC, AND NOT A ROMAN CATHOLIC. A LETTER IN REPLY TO THE REV. R.W. SIBTHORP.

1843, THE NATIONAL RESTORATION OF THE JEWS TO THEIR FATHERLAND, AND CONSEQUENT FULFILMENT OF THE PROMISE TO THE PATRIARCHS. A SERMON ON HEBREWS 11:16 WITH A PRELIMINARY ADDRESS BY H.I.D.

1843, A VISIT TO MY FATHER LAND, BEING NOTES OF A JOURNEY TO SYRIA AND PALESTINE IN1843.

1845-47, קול ישראל THE VOICE OF ISRAEL. CONDUCTED BY JEWS WHO BELIEVE IN JESUS OF NAZARETH AS THE MESSIAH. EDITED BY THE REV. R.H. HERSCHELL. VOL. 1, 2.

1846, PSALMS AND HYMNS FOR CONGREGATIONAL WORSHIP. SELECTED BY RIDLEY H. HERSCHELL.

1848, JEWISH WITNESSES; THAT JESUS IS THE CHRIST. EDITED BY R.H. HERSCHELL.

1848, THE MYSTERY OF THE GENTILE DISPENSATION, AND THE WORK OF THE MESSIAH.

1856, A VISIT TO MY FATHER LAND, BEING NOTES OF A JOURNEY TO SYRIA AND PALESTINE. WITH ADDITIONAL NOTES OF A JOURNEY IN 1854.

1858, THE GOLDEN LAMP: AN EXPOSITION OF THE TABERNACLE AND ITS SERVICES.

1860, STRENGTH IN WEAKNESS. MEDITATIONS ON SOME OF THE PSALMS, BY R.H.H.

Published Works of Helen S. Herschell

1835, THE CHILD'S HELP TO SELF-EXAMINATION AND PRAYER.

1839, A VOICE FROM THE FIRE

1842, FIRE-SIDE HARMONY; OR, DOMESTIC RECREATION IN PART SINGING; A SELECTION OF OLD GLEES…ARRANGED TO WORDS SUITABLE FOR FAMILIES AND SCHOOLS

Published Works of Ghetal Herschell (G.B. Sanderson)

1854, FAR ABOVE RUBIES, MEMOIRS OF H.S.H. BY HER DAUGHTER. EDITED BY R.H. HERSCHELL. (THE BYSTANDER, BY MRS HERSCHELL).

Other sources

THE EDINBURGH ALMANACK OR UNIVERSAL SCOTS & IMPERIAL REGISTER FOR 1823, Oliver & Boyd, Edinburgh, 1822

Anderson, Gerald H. (Editor), BIOGRAPHICAL DICTIONARY OF CHRISTIAN MISSIONS, William B. Eerdmans Publishing Company, 1998

Binney, Thomas, A FUNERAL SERMON ON THE OCCASION OF THE DEATH OF THE LATE RIDLEY H. HERSCHELL: PREACHED IN TRINITY CHAPEL, JOHN STREET, EDGWARE ROAD, 1864

Brown, Stewart J., THOMAS CHALMERS AND THE GODLY COMMONWEALTH IN SCOTLAND, Oxford University Press, 1982

Bundock, John F., OLD LEIGH, A PICTORIAL HISTORY, Biddles Ltd., Guildford and Kings Lynn, 1978

Burdon-Sanderson (Ghetal, Lady), SIR JOHN BURDON SANDERSON, A MEMOIR COMPLETED AND EDITED BY HIS NEPHEW AND NIECE WITH A SELECTION FROM HIS PAPERS, Oxford, Clarendon Press, 1911

Dodsworth, William, REMARKS ON THE SECOND LETTER OF R.W. SIBTHORP ENTITLED "A FURTHER ANSWER TO THE ENQUIRY, WHY HAVE YOU BECOME A CATHOLIC?", London 1842

Dunlop, John, MEMOIR OF GOSPEL TRIUMPHS AMONG THE JEWS DURING THE VICTORIAN ERA, S.W. Partridge & Co., 9 Paternoster Row, John Snow & Co., Ivy Lane, Paternoster Row, 1894

Fuller-Maitland, Caroline, HOW WE WENT TO ROME IN 1857, The Leadenhall Press Ltd., 1892

Fuller-Maitland J.A., A DOOR-KEEPER OF MUSIC, John Murray, Albermarle Street, London, 1929

Galbraith, Ian B., A VILLAGE HERITAGE, THE PARISH OF RHU (1648-1980), Rhu & Shandon Kirk Session, 1981

Gartenhaus, Jacob, FAMOUS HEBREW CHRISTIANS, Baker Book House Company, 1979

Hopkins, Mary Alden, HANAH MORE AND HER CIRCLE, Longmans, Green & Co., 39 Paternoster Row, London, 1947

Johnson, S.F., MICHAEL TOMLIN, A FISHER OF MEN, John Burrows & Sons Ltd, Southend-on-Sea, 1945

Meyer, Louis, EMINENT HEBREW CHRISTIANS OF THE 19TH CENTURY, 1904

O'Rorke, L.E., LIFE AND FRIENDSHIPS OF CATHERINE MARSH, Longmans, Green & Co., 39 Paternoster Row, London, 1917

Pryor Hack, Mary, SELF-SURRENDER: A SECOND SERIES OF "CONSECRATED WOMEN", Hodder and Stoughton, 1887

Romano, Terrie M., MAKING MEDICINE SCIENTIFIC: JOHN BURDON SANDERSON AND THE CULTURE OF VICTORIAN SCIENCE, The John Hopkins University Press, 2002

Wilks, Michael (Editor), STUDIES IN CHURCH HISTORY, SUBSIDIA 10, PROPHECY AND ESCHATOLOGY, Blackwell Publishers, 1994

Williams, Judith, LEIGH-ON-SEA, A HISTORY, The Cromwell Press, Trowbridge, 2002

For further information contact the author on info@htsmedia.com